This I Trust

Basic Words of Christian Belief

Wolfgang Huber

Translated by Margaret Kohl

**World Council
of Churches**
Publications

THIS I TRUST
Basic Words of Christian Belief

WCC Publications is the book publishing programme of the World Council of Churches. Founded in 1948, the WCC promotes Christian unity in faith, witness and service for a just and peaceful world. A global fellowship, the WCC brings together more than 349 Protestant, Orthodox, Anglican and other churches representing more than 560 million Christians in 110 countries and works cooperatively with the Roman Catholic Church.

Opinions expressed in WCC Publications are those of the authors.

Scripture quotations are from the New Revised Standard Version Bible, © copyright 1989 by the Division of Christian Education of the National Council of the Churches of Christ in the USA. Used by permission.

Cover design: Adele Robey/Phoenix Graphics, Inc.
Cover image: iStock
Book design and typesetting: 4 Seasons Book Design/Michelle Cook
ISBN: 978-2-8254-1579-5

World Council of Churches
150 route de Ferney, P.O. Box 2100
1211 Geneva 2, Switzerland
http://publications.oikoumene.org

Contents

Introduction:
The Beginning

❀

Who am I?
How do I engage with other people?
What am I sure about?

❀

Everyone asks these three questions. We all search for the answers.

Who am I? This question has accompanied me all my life. It can't be answered in a single sentence. My identity has many facets. Not everything I find important can be seen or made evident. As human beings our questions reach beyond ourselves. That is the only way in which we can understand who we are. We look for some support that we cannot give ourselves. In order for us to accept and affirm the finitude of our lives, our hope has to extend beyond our life's end. We need a clear compass if we are not to leave the way free for our egoism and our dislike for other people.

How do I engage with other people? No one lives in isolation. No one is born without a mother. We all live together with others. To meet them openly, to develop stable relationships, to forgive, and to clear away misunderstandings—all these things have to be learned.

The world we live in is becoming more diverse and motley. Our society is marked by a multiplicity—indeed a clash—of attitudes and ways of behaving. We live together with people who are very different from each other. To ignore them or to keep them at a hostile arm's length is no solution. But to accept them and still remain true to ourselves is not always easy. We have to be open and tolerant toward other people's convictions, but at the same time we need a clear position of our own, a reliable orientation.

What am I sure about? We look for a place of our own among all the confused voices of the religions and philosophies. In Europe, and especially in Germany, a considerable measure of religious indifference has become widespread. But in the clash between secular attitudes, the increasing strength of Islam, and an often cloudy Christianity, many people feel that they themselves need clarity. Some are demanding a Christian "core culture." Others are rediscovering "the Christian West," although "the decline of the West" was already a theme about a hundred years ago.

Phrases of this kind sound like an invocation of "the good old days." But the Christian faith is more than a cultural heritage. It is only alive when it becomes the power for living and puts its stamp on a person's outlook. But let us be honest: many people are no longer clear about what distinguishes the Christian faith from other religions or secular attitudes. We can find clarity about this if we come to understand what the central testimonies of the Christian faith are.

Most people receive the essential stamp for the whole of their lives in their earliest childhood. Naturally, we cannot remember our very first years, but it is then that we form the foundational convictions we carry with us from that point onward, as a matter of course. Consequently, it doesn't ever occur to most people to call their sustaining convictions into question. And to change these convictions is correspondingly hard. We live from a basic trust and draw on that trust throughout life. Sometimes we are asked what this trust is. We ought to be able to tell our questioners, for many people do not possess any certainty of this kind. For them, important questions are unsolved. For them, what was made accessible to them in their earliest youth no longer exists. They are searching. They are prepared to discover new bearings. Can the Christian faith be a help to them? How can it acquire the power to convince?

First, undoubtedly, through people who live this faith, through models from whom one can take one's bearings. Those who meet people like this, or are impressed by models of this kind, go on to ask more. They ask about the substance of what these people believe. They want to learn the language of faith. They want to understand the most important tenets of faith, and to grapple with these central assertions for themselves. I am convinced that today many people are not content with general religious assertions, with commonplace pronouncements about what is right, or with banal platitudes. They are looking for spiritual depth, spiritual content, clarity in questions of faith.

Today, for reasons like this, we are asking afresh about key texts of Christian faith. What are the important, the really basic sayings? No one can develop an equally intensive relationship to the whole multiplicity of the biblical testimonies or to the wealth of two thousand years of Christian witness. We all select. Some people have only a slender store of familiar biblical verses, hymns, and prayers. Other people have a greater treasury on which to draw. But we all need sources for our own spirituality, sources that will let us grow in faith and stand firm in doubt.

We can only approach these sources with the courage to select. Every selection is subjective, but that does not mean that it is fortuitous. Every selection dispenses with things that are important, but that does not make what is chosen unimportant. I, too, would have liked to add many other texts to the ones in this book, but I did not want to leave out any of the ones I have chosen. In this little book I am drawing attention to key texts in the Bible and in Christian tradition that can be an aid to faith in the 21st century. Each of the texts is important in my own life and for my own faith, and this experience allows me to hope that they may help others, too. In the following 14 chapters I describe what these texts mean to me, and the contexts they illuminate for me. Out of these elements a picture of Christian faith will come together before the eyes of the reader.

My viewpoint is consciously ecumenical. Faith in Jesus Christ is not Protestant or Catholic, nor is it Orthodox or free church; it is Christian faith. But at the same time my viewpoint is consciously Protestant, because I am convinced that we don't learn to believe, and remain believers, in a vacuum; we do so in the context of a specific community. So in addition to biblical sources and texts from the early Christian era, insights stemming from the time of the Reformation make their contribution, as well as voices of Protestant Christians down to our own time.

In this book I am describing the things I trust and which I hope other people will also find trustworthy. Each chapter begins with one or two texts taken from the Bible, from the hymnbook, or from the tradition of Christian thinking. The biblical texts are taken from the New Revised Standard Version. My own comments build the bridge to questions of our own time. They are an invitation to readers to find their own answers, and to enter into conversation with others who together are engaged in the same search.

1. Faith Is a Matter of Trust

The LORD is my shepherd, I shall not want.
He makes me lie down in green pastures;
he leads me beside still waters;
he restores my soul.
He leads me in right paths
for his name's sake.

Even though I walk through the darkest valley,
I fear no evil;
for you are with me;
your rod and your staff—
they comfort me.

You prepare a table before me
in the presence of my enemies;
you anoint my head with oil;
my cup overflows.
Surely goodness and mercy shall follow me
all the days of my life,
and I shall dwell in the house of the LORD
my whole life long.
—*Psalm 23*

Safekeeping in the Words of the Psalms

I have known Psalm 23 as long as I can remember. When I try to find words for the trust that sustains me, I often turn to the words of this psalm. When my mother lay dying, I prayed Psalm 23 with her. She found talking difficult, but she spoke it with me. When I stood beside my wife at her mother's deathbed, we prayed these words for her, and were sure that the psalm's certainty reached her. This is about a trust that stands firm at the limits of life.

It is not only in personal life that we come up against limits of this kind. We encounter them in social and political life, too. On 11 September 2001 a shock spread with the force of a sudden blast when two aircraft crashed into the twin towers of the World Trade Center in New York, killing thousands of people. That evening, a huge crowd gathered at the cathedral in Berlin; many people could not get in and waited patiently outside the doors of the church. We had to find words out of the shock of the moment, and our own words could not provide the support that was now needed. We took refuge in the language of the Bible, above all Psalm 23, the psalm of trust. And many people prayed with us.

The psalms are part of the Old Testament, the Holy Scripture of Judaism. But they have an important place in the Christian Bible, too. The first copy of the New Testament I can remember included the psalter as well. For the psalms are the Bible's prayerbook. In religious communities, where the pattern of daily life is shaped by times of prayer, a psalm, said or sung antiphonally, belongs to the morning, midday, and evening prayers. Praying the psalm for the week is also a firm component in Sunday worship.

The psalms cover varying situations in human life. They give expression to praise and lament, thanksgiving and consolation. For thousands of years men and women have used the words of the psalter as a way of bringing their own situations and their own feelings before God. Many of the psalms provide words for the experience of men and women who have felt God's guidance in the profoundest peril. In the psalms, trust in God finds a voice.

Trust in God

Trust is not the opposite of challenge and doubt. It is precisely in doubt that trust finds its strength. It preserves this strength in the face of new questions. Trust does not prove itself by being able to provide someone with an answer to the theoretical question of where evil comes from. It shows itself in the fact that it does not capitulate even in the face of evil.

The language of the psalms helps us to accept the finitude of our lives. This finitude does not emerge for the first time at the end of life, but is evident from the very beginning.

None of us knows why we are living at this particular moment. None of us can arrange the time and hour of his or her birth. That is still true even if one's parents planned when they would like to have a child. None of us can determine the time and hour of our death. That is still true, even if today some people cut their lives short, or hope that the doctor will help them in their dying.

It is not only when it is a matter of life's beginning or its end that we sense the finitude of our lives. Even in the midst of life we have only limited possibilities. Our powers are restricted; we can merely choose between certain options, and it is often only through hindsight that we grasp which the right one would have been.

Sometimes we long for unlimited freedom, but we know in our heart of hearts that without restriction there is neither freedom nor happiness. We commit ourselves to a particular person. The fact that we came to know that person could not be foreseen. In faithfulness to each other we experience an incomparable fulfilment; but at the same time we know how fragile this supreme good of a shared life is.

When they are asked on their birthday about their most important wish for the new year ahead, many people reply, "Good health—that is the most important thing." Because none of us can guarantee one's own health, and because no doctor can ensure permanent health, we have to wish health for ourselves and for other people. We raise our glasses and say, "Good health!" The French say, "*Santé!*" In Germany, when someone sneezes the other responds with the same wish, saying *Gesundheit*! ("good health").

Every living organism can become sick. Illness is part of human life. The wish for good health expresses the hope for preservation from illness, and the prayer for a speedy recovery. But the prayer for health can also be replaced by the prayer for God's consoling Spirit, so that we can accept sickness and death.

When we pray, the uncertainties of our lives become endurable. It is not just the beginning and the end of life over which we have no control. The same is true of the midst of life—its happiness, its fulfilment. If we trust in God we can endure the uncertainties, accept the limitations, and receive the fullness of life as a gift.

Images of Trust

The psalms do not just awaken this trust through general assertions about who God is and what God does. They bring this trust close to us by way of powerful images. In Psalm 23 two images are linked. We meet God as the good shepherd, who leads us to the source of life and wards off danger. And God also shows Godself as the good host, whose goodness puts the threatening powers and forces in their place. The safekeeping that God confers reaches beyond the frontiers of life: "Goodness and mercy shall follow me all the days of my life, and I shall dwell in the house of the LORD forever." These words are the expression of a promise that doesn't end with the close of life. According to this and many other translations of the Bible, it endures not just "lifelong" but "forever."

The early Christian community often depicted Jesus Christ as the good shepherd who carries a sheep on his shoulders so as to bring it to safety. In the dejected people Jesus met, he awakened trust: "Your faith has helped you. Go in peace." To the weary and heavy-laden he promises refreshment. He renews the security we have with God through committing his life. The certainty that God has a loving purpose for us frees us to look into the future. The trust that bears us up is centred in the certainty that with God we are in safekeeping.

Abraham and his faith have become the archetypal image for this; that is why we are told about it near the beginning of the Bible (Exodus 12ff.). Abraham leaves his own country, cuts himself off from all his relatives, and sets out on a path with an uncertain end. He sets out in the confidence that God has some good purpose for him. That is why he doesn't stay in the country familiar to him, and doesn't content himself with what he had always known. He embarks on something new.

Trust and Trustworthiness

Trust must not be confused with that which we regard as trustworthy because it is familiar and has always been what it is now. Trust knows how to cope with change. Trustworthiness in the sense of familiarity should not be disparaged. The fact that we feel at home in particular place is a great blessing. What is "trusty" gives us security. But that should not be confused with trust. For trust is directed toward the future. Abraham's trust is not just that in trust he stops short, but that he is certain of God's good guidance.

That is why, for Jews, Christians, and Muslims, Abraham's setting forth from the land of his forefathers has become a primal image of faith. He took on himself the greatest of insecurities, yet his faith was stronger still. The promise that even difficulties would be transformed into blessings went with him. "You shall be a blessing." That a trust of this kind can be a blessing for others is the fundamental experience of faith: "You shall be a blessing."

Anyone who lives from a trust like this hopes for good things from God: "The Lord is my shepherd, I shall not want." It is not by chance that great models of faith have continually dared new beginnings of the kind the Bible describes in the figure of Abraham. The Nobel Prize–winner Albert Schweitzer (1875–1965) is an example. He broke out of his successful career as a renowned theologian and organist and became a doctor in order to help people in Africa who until then had not been reached by modern medicine. In this new start oriented toward the needy he perceived what he was called to do.

When values change, trust is called in question, too. "Trust is good, control is better"—this tenet is often quoted, although its author, Vladimir Lenin, the first leader of the Bolshevist Soviet revolution, is admittedly for many people no more than a name. People count the person who trusts others as gullible, a judgment as disparaging as the description "well-meaning." Today the label is pinned to people who believe that the world can be influenced by moral values. Of course, trust can be misused, and the hope that the world can be changed in the direction of the good, and through the good, can founder. But that is no reason for mocking trust and moral steadfastness and for bringing them into disrepute. For both of them are irreplaceable.

For that reason, the mistrust of trust is one of the great errors of our time. In no sphere of activity does the indispensability of trust emerge more clearly than in economic life. The relationship between supplier and customer, or the transactions between banks, rests on trust. If trust is squandered or withdrawn, the consequence is as ruinous as if what was missing were money. The great global financial crisis of 2007 to 2009 was at heart a crisis of trust. The giant protective umbrellas, with the billions expended on them by governments in this crisis, are supposed to provide a substitute for the trust that has been lost. But for trust there is no substitute. To disparage trust is quite mistaken.

What is decisive, of course, is not the trust we put in other people, important though that is. If what we are asking about is a foundation for our lives that will stand the test, it is even less merely a matter of self-trust, indispensible though that, too, is. We only arrive at a firm foundation for our lives when we put ultimate trust not in ourselves and other people but in God. That God is the anchor of our trust is the essential substance of faith.

Neither self-trust nor trust in other people extends beyond life itself. Trust of this kind is limited and provisional. It does not renew itself from our own strength; it needs a basis that is more firmly rooted than that. Only faith in God provides a basis for renewing trust in other people, and for not foundering, in view of the limitations that are set to our self-trust. Trust in God is a power for living that cannot be put on the same level as self-trust or as trust in other people. Trust in God is the root from which everything else can grow.

2. The Gift of Life

❀

I believe in God,
the Father Almighty,
maker of heaven and earth.
—*The Apostles' Creed, 2nd to 4th century CE, First Article*

I believe that God has created me together with all living creatures,
that he has given me and still sustains
my body and soul, eyes, ears, and all my members,
my reason and all my senses;
has given me clothing and shoes, food and drink,
hearth and home, wife and child,
fields, cattle, and all I possess;
that he provides for me abundantly and daily
with all that is needful for body and life,
protects me in all danger,
and guards and preserves me from all evil;
and that all this he does out of pure, fatherly, divine goodness and mercy,
without any merit or deserving of mine.
For all this I am bound to thank and praise him,
to serve him and obey him.
This is assuredly true.
—*Martin Luther, Small Catechism, Explanation of the First Article, 1529*

❀

Wonder

The person who believes in God remembers first of all that God created the world. The Hebrew Bible—for Christians the Old Testament—therefore begins with narratives about the creation. And the Apostles' Creed, in which early Christianity summed up its most important convictions, begins with God the Creator. The acknowledgment of Jesus Christ as God's Son, and of the Holy Spirit, follows in the creed's next two articles. But first of all it talks about God the Creator.

The two chapters about creation do not come at the beginning of the Bible simply because they are its earliest texts, for that is by no means the case. They stand at the beginning because they are of fundamental importance for an understanding of the world and life. Similarly, fundamental questions are then the subject of what follows—how evil came into the world, why people attack each other with violence, why the human world is saved in spite of its wickedness, and why there is so much confusion among human beings. All these questions have to do with the ways men and women go astray; but they are all preceded by what is good: God's creation.

We can understand why. Gratitude for life overwhelms everyone who holds a newly born child in her or his arms. In the eyes of this child there lies an open future; what shines on us from these eyes is innocence. Wonder over the miracle of life deserves absolute precedence before all the pondering over threatening dangers, plans that have miscarried, or misguided steps.

What we experience when we look at a newly born child is repeated when we become aware of creation in all its rich and colourful diversity. Children love to visit a zoo. They encounter the variety of the animals. In the garden, or in the woods and fields, they discover the differences between the flowers.

On the beach, they build castles or canals, admire the water that flows through the channels they have built for it, and delight in the shells they find. If they can take a walk and leave behind them the effort of climbing a hill or mountain, they marvel at the expanse of the mountain world.

During the walk a new panorama is continually disclosed and, in the same way, throughout our lives we pass from one astonishment to the next. The surprise grows when we get beyond what we can see with the naked eye. The microscope shows us the wonder of life in the tiniest molecules. The telescope opens up for us a vista into the universe. Our reverence becomes greater still when we perceive that, measured against the vastness of the universe, the earth on which we live is more like a speck of dust. There can be no question of our being at home at the centre of the world. The fact that the earth revolves round the sun does not mean that the sun constitutes the centre of the world, for there are many suns.

Astonishment is the first thing. Gratitude for the wonder of creation is not diminished because modern science opens up for us the mysteries of nature that earlier seemed incomprehensible. The fact that we with our own lives are part of creation astonishes us all the more. Sometime or other, we all ask ourselves why we are in the world at all. How easily I might never have been born! Since I myself am the youngest of five brothers, I have sometimes surmised that the wish for a daughter contributed to my birth. And what if there had no longer been any such wish, after the birth of four sons?

The grateful astonishment over the wonders of creation and over our own lives is the beginning of trust in God. In the face of the majesty of creation, we confess the majesty of God. Because we have to thank God for the universe in which we live and move, we call God "Almighty." That does not mean a capricious almightiness, which can be employed in each case for one's own purposes. What it means is that the whole of the world in which we live is surrounded and interpenetrated by the reality of God.

This conviction led the medieval theologian Anselm of Canterbury to a concept of God that is worth thinking about: God is that than whom nothing greater can be thought. Anselm considered that this clever formulation was a proof of God's existence. But God's existence cannot be proved by means of thought. Here, thought follows on belief. We try to understand what we have grasped in faith; but we cannot get beyond faith by means of thought. Or to put it another way: wonder runs ahead of understanding.

And yet Anselm was right. If we think God, we understand God as the reality that surpasses everything else. God is that than whom nothing greater can be thought.

Relationships

Astonishment over creation and our life within creation gives our trust in God an inward assurance. Belief in creation helps gratitude to find words. It expresses gratitude for the life that has been given me, and for the world in which I am permitted to live. In this gratitude, the trust that God has a good purpose for me and for the world takes on concrete form. To view one's own life and the whole world from the perspective of the good things that God has put there, and which God desires to preserve, is the meaning of belief in creation.

For that reason, creation is talked about first of all in the mode of praise. "O LORD, our Sovereign, how majestic is your name in all the earth!" (Ps. 8:1, 10). That cry frames one of the most important creation psalms in the Bible. At the beginning of the 16th century, the reformer Martin Luther emphatically picked up this note in his exposition of the First Article of the creed. The fact that life and everything I need to live has been given me—that is the reason for being grateful for creation. In these thanks Luther does not merely include creaturely life. I am not just grateful for naked life. Everything I have and need for living is included: "clothing and shoes, food and drink, hearth and home, wife and child, fields, cattle, and all I possess."

This list is based on a rural life, but it is not difficult to translate it into today's conditions: "Clothing and food, home and health, education and work, family and friends, money for daily life and for holidays, freedom from fear and necessity." That is what a list of these good things in creation might look like today. Some people might add other things that they find particularly important—for many, a mobile phone, a computer, television, and a car would have a prominent position on the list.

In all events we know today, just as people knew in Luther's time, that human life can only flourish within a whole interwoven fabric of natural and cultural conditions. We live in relationships; in death we have no relation.

Family bonds, the relationship between friends, and a neighbourliness we can rely on continually prove to be indispensible. For we human beings are beings-in-relationship. Under the dominance of an egotistical attitude to life this fact recedes into the background. But an existence that simply revolves around one's own self is contrary to creation. The biblical creation stories already pinpoint that. They say that human beings have been created to be the image of God. In the cultural environment of the Bible, only kings were viewed as being the image of God; but the person who

reveres God as creator sees all human beings as beings cor-
responding to God.

We can all respond to God's address to us—we can live
responsibly. In addition, the Bible says that we have been created as men and women. The relationship to other people goes
side by side with the relationship to God, and for this the relationship between man and woman is fundamental. Finally,
the Bible reminds us of the task given to us to understand the
world and to shape it.

In our relationship to God, our fellow human beings,
and the world in which we live, we at the same time build
up a relationship to ourselves. We determine our place in the
world surrounding us. For this we use language, which distinguishes human beings even from those closest to them among
the animals. We create a civilization with the help of which
we become at home in our world. We use nature in order to
keep ourselves alive; for we differ from animals in that it is not
enough for us to follow our instincts.

Faith and Science

All these correlations have been investigated by the modern
sciences in far greater detail than was possible in former times.
There is no need to deny that the biblical texts were written in
a prescientific age, the writers still able unreservedly to see the
meaning of creation and the origin of the world as one. Thus
gratitude for the good gifts of the Creator was combined with
stories telling how God created everything at the beginning,
and that it was good.

The variety among such narratives of origin emerges quite
clearly in the Bible. We find two of them, set side by side, in its
first two chapters. The one splits up the work of creation into

a sequence of six days, with the seventh day, the day of rest, as its crowning conclusion. The other views the work of creation entirely from the standpoint of the human being, who is not only part of creation but has a relation to it, since he is charged to till the earth and preserve it (Gen. 2:15).

If two narratives with such different emphases are set parallel to each other, this clearly points to the fact that we must not make the conceptual world of these stories the substance of faith. We must take them for what they are: with the help of the conceptual world of their time, they give visual form to gratitude for the gift of creation. But they abstract many of the magical elements with which this conceptual world was shot through. The Bible does not let the world issue from a struggle between rival gods; it proceeds from the sovereign creative act of the one God. It does not interpret sun, moon, and stars as deities; they are heavenly lights created by God. It does not see human beings as servants of the gods; they are God's image. And it does not view the world as chaos; it is an order wrung by God out of this chaos. So there are three central elements in the biblical idea of creation: the supremacy of the Creator, the dignity of the human being, and the unity of creation.

The scientific theories about the origin of the world and the development of life do not in any way touch this insight into the good meaning of creation. They show what modern science can achieve. The task they have set themselves is to explain nature according to natural laws. They see in nature a complex warp and weft of processes, all linked together through the law of cause and effect, that is to say, through the law of causality. But the causal processes which act on one another in nature are so multifarious that although scientists can retrospectively explain why the outcome was this world and not a different one, they cannot predict the world's further development. In the same way, with the methods of evolutionary theory they can retrospectively explain how living things came into being, and how the human being finally evolved in the long chain of life; but they cannot definitively predict how life will develop. In recent times they have even been able to explain how ideas and decisions come about in the human brain; but they cannot predict what ideas a person will form and the decisions that person will make.

The fact that natural laws are valid does not mean that the future is fixed. Our own personal futures and the future of our world are still open. Each and every one of us contributes to this future, whether it be in personal life or through the sectors for which we are responsible in our jobs or professions. To whom are we responsible for the way we deal with the open future? Ultimately, we are responsible toward the reality that determines us—toward God, who wills that the future will be a good future.

Science and faith are mutually complementary. They open up different views of the reality in which we live: the viewpoints of wonder and of investigation, the viewpoints of gratitude and law, the viewpoints of openness and fixity.

It is not always easy to adapt to such different ways of looking at things. Consequently. it is continually maintained that belief in creation has been confuted by science. Belief in a creator God is held to be incompatible with the insights of modern scientists into the way the world and life came into being. The world has its beginning in time; it does not constitute the beginning of time. And life comes into being on earth in a gradual process of evolution, not in a sudden act of creation. Thus we have the two most important scientific objections.

But these two objections rest on a fundamental misunderstanding. For belief in creation is not a theory about the genesis of the world in the sense of modern science, nor does it compete with new scientific theories about the development of life. It describes the good purpose that is bound up with creation as a whole, and with each of its parts. Science, by contrast, explains with the help of natural laws why the world has become what it now is. Science has to do with the world as it has become, faith with what it is intended to be.

But the conflict between faith and science is also fueled from faith's side. For it is not only scientists who understand the biblical creation stories as being theories about the genesis of the world. A misunderstanding of this kind is also maintained from the side of faith. Belief in creation then becomes a philosophy with the name of creationism. With this philosophy, the proponents of a religious fundamentalism want to defeat evolutionary theory. But a scientific theory can be surmounted only through better science, not through a religious philosophy. And the Christian faith is sold short if it is put forward as a religious worldview with a claim to explain the world.

This debate is unfruitful. What is highly fruitful, however, is to take both insights seriously: the insights of modern science, together with the open questions that arise from them, but equally the trust in creation out of which we can live and act.

3. Rivalry and Respect

Now the man knew his wife Eve, and she conceived and bore Cain, saying, "I have produced a man with the help of the LORD." Next she bore his brother Abel. Now Abel was a keeper of sheep, and Cain a tiller of the ground. In the course of time Cain brought to the LORD an offering of the fruit of the ground, and Abel for his part brought of the firstlings of his flock, their fat portions. And the LORD had regard for Abel and his offering, but for Cain and his offering he had no regard. So Cain was very angry, and his countenance fell. The LORD said to Cain, "Why are you angry, and why has your countenance fallen? If you do well, will you not be accepted? And if you do not do well, sin is lurking at the door; its desire is for you, but you must master it."

Cain said to his brother Abel, "Let us go out to the field." And when they were in the field, Cain rose up against his brother Abel, and killed him. Then the LORD said to Cain, "Where is your brother Abel?" He said, "I do not know. Am I my brother's keeper?" And the LORD said, "What have you done? Listen, your brother's blood is crying out to me from the ground, And now you are cursed from the ground, which has opened its mouth to receive your brother's blood from your hand. When you till the ground, it will no longer yield to you its strength: you will be a fugitive and a wanderer on the earth." Cain said to the LORD, "My punishment is greater than I can bear! Today you have driven me away from the soil, and I shall be a fugitive and wanderer on the earth, and anyone who meets me may kill me." Then the LORD said to him, "Not so! Whoever kills Cain will suffer a sevenfold vengeance." And the LORD put a mark on Cain, so that no one who came upon him would kill him. Then Cain went away from the presence of the LORD, and settled in the land of Nod, east of Eden.

Cain knew his wife, and she conceived and bore Enoch: and he built a city, and named it Enoch after his son Enoch. To Enoch was born Irad; and Irad was the father of Mehujael, and Mehujael the father of Lamech. Lamech took two wives; the name of the one was Adah, and the name of the other Zillah. Adah bore Jabal; he was the ancestor of those who live in tents and have livestock. His brother's name was Jubal; he was the ancestor of those who play the lyre and pipe. Zillah bore Tubal-cain, who made all kinds of bronze and iron tools. The sister of Tubal-cain was Naamah.

> Lamech said to his wives:
> "Adah and Zillah, hear my voice;
> you wives of Lamech, listen to what I say;
> I have killed a man for wounding me,
> a young man for striking me.
> If Cain is avenged sevenfold,
> truly Lamech seventy-sevenfold."

Adam knew his wife again, and she bore a son and named him Seth, for she said, "God has appointed for me another child instead of Abel, because Cain killed him." To Seth also a son was born, and he named him Enosh. At that time people began to invoke the name of the LORD.

—*Genesis 4:1-26*

Rivalry and Violence

The story of Cain and Abel brings us face to face with human history in all its ambiguity. In this mirror, the conflicting character of our own lives is reflected in their dividedness. Instead of facing up to this, readers of this story have generally made the two brothers Cain and Abel the symbols of an all-too-simple pattern. Guilt has been assigned to the one side, and righteousness to the other. Abel has been viewed as the just man and Cain as the sinner; Abel the innocent victim and Cain the man of violence—no further questions. Readers put themselves on Abel's side, sending Cain into the wilderness, into the land of Nod, beyond Eden.

This widespread reaction to the biblical story about Cain and Abel is understandable. We can enter into it not just because it exonerates us. For a short while, at least, having a scapegoat makes us feel better. This reaction is all the more plausible because there is no excuse for what Cain does. He commits the cruelest act possible among human beings. In murderous violence, he takes the life of his brother and rival. Because Abel was successful, he stood in his brother's way, and Cain the farmer, "the tiller of the ground," even cries cynically after the shepherd, "Am I my brother's keeper?"

The story shows how violence springs up out of the rivalry between people. This rivalry develops such a primitive dynamic that even God's authority cannot do anything against it. And in this way the story of Cain and Abel shows simultaneously how violence springs from rebellion against God. The separation from God and the separation from one's neighbour are closely connected.

The story of Cain and Abel shows how this double separation comes about even more typically than does the story about Adam and Eve in paradise, the famous story of the fall. In the primal history told in the Bible, which runs from creation to the building of tower of Babel (Genesis 1–11), these two stories describe in different ways how a human life gets off track once a person turns away from God. But the story of Cain and Abel doesn't bring us into a paradisal setting; this is an everyday conflict. It doesn't tell us about temptation by a serpent; it tells us how hate arises. The hand reaches out, not for an apple from the Tree of Knowledge, but for a murderous weapon. Cain raises his hand against his brother and strikes him dead. Anyone who is sure that he or she could never commit such a murderous act is reminded by Jesus in the Sermon on the Mount that killing starts in the heart, and begins with the contemptuous word (Matt. 5:21f.). How quickly we say to someone—or at least think it—"I could kill you!"

Cain brings us face to face with a primal picture of what happens if we see our fellow human beings only as rivals and competitors, and forget that God loves them in just the same way as God loves us. If we give way to the rivalry, and resort to violence against other people, we cannot proffer any excuse. That was so then, and is still the case today. There is no heavier guilt. Unsettled and volatile, we wander about restlessly outside Eden.

Someone Loved by God

There is no possible excuse for killing another person. That explains the partisanship for Abel. Nevertheless, I will not adopt the usual stance, in which the brothers are contrasted with each other, the righteous Abel and Cain the sinner. I won't play along with the game that drives Cain again and again into the wilderness—as a scapegoat, who lets us forget our own sins. No, I will put myself on Cain's side. For I am closer to him, the perpetrator, than I am to Abel, the victim.

At first sight it seems to us not merely unjust but incomprehensible: Cain has descendants; Abel's life, in contrast, remains in the literal sense of the word fruitless. Cain becomes the builder of the first city, which he calls Enoch after his first son. But the cattle breeders are also Cain's descendants, since the shepherd Abel has no children. It is also explicitly stressed that the musicians and smiths are descended from Cain. All this would be somehow incomprehensible if there were nothing to be said about Cain except that he was a murderer.

There is no way around it. We have to establish that this same Cain was also someone whom God loved. When he is born his mother greets him proudly, with the words, "I have produced a man with the help of God" (Gen. 4:1). Even if it is won through pain, she experiences the great gift that we are permitted to pass life on to a succeeding generation. It is a pattern that is repeated down to the present day.

Cain: someone God loved. He is given a brother, so he that he doesn't have to grow up alone. He has a companion. This is how all human society begins. Life develops in many strands. A division of labour is possible, as it was between Abel, the "keeper of sheep," and Cain, who farmed the soil. There is no need for everyone to do the same thing, for we are not alone. We can work together and by doing so achieve more than would be possible for any one of us just by ourselves.

If only it were not for the rivalry, that fatal tendency to set oneself up against the other, instead of sharing life together! If only we did not have the need to distinguish ourselves at the cost of other people, instead of making life with one another our common profile! If it were not for our propensity to magnify ourselves by putting other people down, life could really blossom.

Cain surrenders to the rivalry in full. His brother is successful, he is unsuccessful; the one enjoys recognition, the other is pushed into the background; the one is lucky, the other is unlucky. These differences are inexplicable. That is the root of the rivalry that ends in violence and murder. Cain looks for someone who is responsible for what is inexplicable; and with that the disaster takes its course. He wants a complete explanation for this seeming injustice, and thus what he himself brings about is injustice.

And yet: God loves this Cain, too. When hate boils up in Cain, God warns him. God encourages Cain to see things clearly. The clear view sees in the other person a being whom God has also created. The clear view seeks for reconciliation in the conflict. But even after Cain has proved to be incapable of this view, God does not give him up. Instead, God also appeals to the murderer's responsibility: "Where is your brother?" God considers the man of violence worthy of this question, which shows the indestructible nature of human dignity. "Where is your brother?" This question can be liberating, a way out of despair. God considers us, in all our violence, worthy of another word.

Cain ignores this call. He asks sneeringly if he is then supposed to look after his brother. What older brothers and sisters usually have no desire for, he also rejects: responsibility for the smaller ones. But this time the refusal has deadly consequences. The danger to the younger brother does not threaten him from outside. It is the older brother himself, in his hurt pride, who takes his brother's life, with terrible consequences for himself as well. He can never again shake off his blood guilt for what he has done to his brother.

The murderer does not escape this curse. But even as someone cursed, he is not forsaken by God. God saves his life, even after the act of murder. Cain is given a sign on his forehead. This "mark of Cain" is not the token of a curse, as a superficial interpretation would have it. It is a mark of preservation. The consequences of the guilt he has incurred do not recoil on him. He is mercifully preserved.

God saves the life of the murderer, the sinner. God raises up the person who has failed. God awakens the culture of concern to new life. It is not Cain who rules the world but God, so even Cain can live. But the mark of preservation is ours as well. Without God's grace we should be helplessly delivered up to our own guilt.

Being Each Other's Keeper

Cain sneeringly rejects the question about his brother: "Am I my brother's keeper?" But this reaction shows all the more clearly what we human beings are destined for. We are not made to hate our brothers and sisters but to care for them. This is the essential precondition for a shared life.

In the light of this insight, we must continually critically examine our own lives and the shared life of society. In a time that threatens to be drawn into the undertow of a cold-hearted egoism, we must attach a special value to the counterforces. At a time when some people are smiled on by the god of the market, while others only achieve very little and so count as worthless, we must once more learn that we are intended to be each other's keepers; we must not let each other drop. It is only then that there can be a successful future in solidarity and justice.

If we are to understand the end of this story, we must always remember that Cain is someone whom God loves. Cain becomes the father of an advanced civilization, the builder of the first city, the forefather of musicians and smiths. Achievements are traced back to him without which a culturally fulfilled and secure life would be inconceivable: a shared life within the walls of a town, full of the sound of music, secured by the work of the smiths.

Abel's life is ended by his brother's violence. In Cain, life goes on—Cain, the man God loves, the murderer out of greedy rivalry, the graciously preserved sinner, the builder of the first city. He thus becomes the symbol of a reconciliation that reaches beyond the abysses of guilt. The person who remembers him should not forget the mark of Cain, the mark of merciful preservation for someone who has become guilty. For Christians, another sign shines out of this one; for them it is the cross which is the sign of merciful preservation, the sign of reconciliation.

The Beginning of Religion

The biblical description of how life continues and develops beyond the abyss of deadly violence has yet another point, which is frequently overlooked. Hardly anyone remembers the end of this biblical story: Adam and Eve have another child, their third. The end is not the pain over Abel's death. Seth is born; his son is called Enosh.

Only then does the story of Cain and Abel come to an end, with the sentence: "At this time the name of the LORD began to be invoked." The history of humanity is not just a history of human violence. There is also a history of humanity's relationship to God. Human beings are not conscious of their relation to God from the outset. They do not give expression to their relationship to God from the very beginning. It takes time before human beings are in a position to turn to God. It is true that from the beginning God speaks to human beings. When Adam hides himself from God, God addresses him with a question: "Where are you, Adam?" He asks Cain, the slayer of his brother, "Where is your brother?" But it is only as time goes on that people learn to turn to God themselves.

Religion has a history. It is part of human culture. The ways in which human beings turn to God change, and there the biblical religion plays a large part. The clarity with which it turned away from the sacrificial cult was an essential contribution toward establishing the prohibition of killing within religion itself. Believers have no reason to deny that religion changes in the course of history.

Fear of this change is a poor counsellor. The point is, rather, to become consciously aware of the change. This emerges particularly clearly in ethical questions: obvious examples are the relation of the Christian churches to human rights and peace, or to sexuality and partnership. But it is not just ethical ideas that are subject to change. The same is true of ideas about God. Later in this book we shall look at this from the aspect of the image of God as the Judge of the world. It is good that this idea has changed since the Middle Ages. But as the story about Cain and Abel shows, the Bible itself already tells about a development of the relationship of human beings to God.

Soon after the story about Abel and Cain, we find in the book of Genesis another story about brothers. It is the story about Abraham and Lot, the two nomads who pasture their flocks of sheep and goats on poor land. As long as their grazing areas are close together, this continually leads to conflict. So they decide that each brother should go his own way, the one to the right hand, the other to the left. At the same time, they don't want to lose sight of each other, "for we are kindred," says Abraham in explanation; "brothers," say some translations (Gen. 13:8). He means that they want to be within reach of each other, even though at a distance. They want to solve the quarrel by keeping more space between them. For this is God's promise: that even outside Eden human beings can live together. And that life in God's name can succeed.

4. Legend and Truth

In those days a decree went out from Emperor Augustus that all the world should be registered. This was the first registration and was taken while Quirinius was governor of Syria. All went to their own towns to be registered. Joseph also went from the town of Nazareth in Galilee to Judea, to the city of David called Bethlehem, because he was descended from the house and family of David. He went to be registered with Mary, to whom he was engaged and who was expecting a child. And she gave birth to her firstborn son and wrapped him in bands of cloth, and laid him in a manger, because there was no place for them in the inn.

In that region there were shepherds in the fields, keeping watch over their flocks by night. Then an angel of the Lord stood before them, and the glory of the Lord shone around them, and they were terrified. But the angel said to them, "Do not be afraid; for see—I am bringing you good news of great joy for all the people: to you is born this day in the city of David a Saviour, who is the Messiah, the Lord. This will be a sign for you: you will find a child wrapped in bands of cloth and lying in a manger. And suddenly there was with the angel a multitude of the heavenly host, praising God and saying,

> "Glory to God in the highest heaven,
> and on earth peace among those whom he favours."

When the angels had left them and gone into heaven, the shepherds said to one another, "Let us now go to Bethlehem and see this thing that

has taken place, which the Lord has made known to us." So they went
with haste and found Mary and Joseph, and the child lying in a manger.
When they saw this, they made known what had been told them about
this child; and all who heard it were amazed at what the shepherds told
them. But Mary treasured all these words and pondered them in her
heart. The shepherds returned, glorifying and praising God for all they
had heard and seen, as it had been told them.

  —*Luke 2:1-20*

The Three-Part Christmas Story

The first biblical text I learned by heart was this one. No
festival brought us children so close to what the Bible has
passed down to us as when we celebrated the Christmas
story. Compared with Christmas, Easter was celebrated
almost like a pagan nature festival. Spring arrived, we could
look for Easter eggs in the garden. But Christmas clearly had
to do with the Bible, and beneath the Christmas tree three
of us five brothers had to recite by heart the biblical story
about the birth of Jesus. Christmas poems and Christmas
carols followed.

On Christmas Eve we recited the Christmas story in three
parts, so in this way we came to see how artistically the story
is constructed.

It starts with the road to Bethlehem taken by the young
couple, Mary and Joseph. This part reaches its climax with the
birth of the child in an inhospitable place.

The second part centres on the proclamation to the shepherds. The circumstances in which the shepherds hear the
angels' message are described as sparsely as possible, for
everything points forward to the message itself: "Today a

Saviour is born to you." This message is followed by the echo in the angelic choir: "Glory to God in the highest heaven and on earth peace and goodwill towards men."

The third part tells how the shepherds make their way to the manger. They marvel at the wonder which, looked at superficially, is utterly without glamour—the birth in a manger, the Saviour of the world in a stable.

The threefold division of this story is both simple and beautiful. That comes out most clearly when it is read aloud. But it has become rare for it to be read by a grown-up in front of the Christmas tree, and rarer still for children to recite it by heart. Rather, one hears it read by a priest or pastor in church, or perhaps as part of a children's nativity play. But for all that, the story is also present in many homes at Christmas time. A crib brings the Christmas Gospel close, the star of Bethlehem adorns the branches of the Christmas tree. Sometimes a Christmas carol is actually sung, not just heard over an audio speaker.

And above all, everywhere there are angels. Apart from guardian angels, Christmas angels are the favourite form of angel devotion. It has been said that in Germany more people believe in angels than believe in God. And yet angels are nothing but God's messengers. The question whether we have to believe in angels as well as in God does not arise. We don't have to acknowledge their independent existence as God's messengers apart from God. They embody the confidence that God's goodness reaches us. They make it easier to listen to God's truth.

Christ the Redeemer Is Here

The Christmas message tells us that God's truth takes on human form, as a child in the manger—whether this manger stood in a stable or in a grotto, as visitors to Bethlehem are still shown at the present day.

The story about Jesus' birth has acquired legendary features. That is not surprising. Today, too, we usually embroider our most important memories, and we do so all the more the oftener we have a reason for telling them. Embellishments of this kind underline the importance the particular event has for us. Many additional figures make up today's nativity plays, and many female shepherds pay tribute, on Christmas Eve, too, to the equal position of men and women; but compared with all this, the Christmas story told in the Bible is actually as brief and clear as possible.

The story proclaims freedom from fear. For we are permitted to know that we are in safekeeping, kept within the saving love of God. This love comes in person, as the unprotected child who needs the help of others. The becoming-human of the "Adam" we hear about in the creation story is surpassed and caught up into the becoming-human of God. Here God shows God's human face, and this human face is the pledge and guarantor of God's lovingkindness toward human beings. "Christ the Redeemer is here," we sing in a Christmas carol— the surety of God's kindness toward human beings. God still stands by us, even though God would have had reason enough to let us go. That is the heart of the Christian faith. God shows God's self in the manger just as God does on the cross. There is no antithesis between the two; there is an intimate connection. It is senseless to play off the manger and the cross against one another. The two reveal the same thing: that the heart of the Christian faith is the becoming-human of God, and in this happening we see God's lovingkindness toward human beings.

For this the Christmas story uses the most powerful religious symbols of the time: the image of the Messiah who at the end of time leads the world to God, and the image of the virgin who gives birth to the Son of God. These images move us deeply today, too. But we are permitted to understand them as parables, and do not have to assume that the birth of Jesus took place in a different way from any other birth. For every birth is a miracle before which we stand reverently, as the shepherds did in front of the manger with the child. Incidentally, the Christmas story in Luke does not see Mary as a "virgin," but as a young married woman. In the New Testament we already find the two statements side by side.

The newborn child is presented as Saviour, that is to say, as the Redeemer and Messiah. But the child in the manger by no means conforms to the way people pictured such a Saviour at that time. For the most important thing about a Messiah was his imposing appearance and stance. His glorious future was evident from the circumstances of his birth. So what people expected in this case was a birth in splendour, not in simplicity.

Yet the simplicity of Jesus' birth cannot be surpassed. It is explicitly dated as taking place during the reign of the emperor Augustus, who was also worshipped as saviour and lord of the world. But the child who comes into the world in such wretched conditions is set in sharp contrast to Augustus. The God who has become human does not appear supported by a terrifying escort, or with glittering symbols of power. His divine purity is shown in poverty and lowliness. And everyone senses that in this way God's closeness to us is shown much more clearly than it would be in grandiose pomp.

It is in line with this simplicity that the first people who are allowed to see the newly born Messiah should be shepherds. They belong to the simple people. They are exposed to wind and weather, and know the daily trials of the poor. Who could testify more convincingly than these people that the Saviour came into the world in a place where otherwise only animals seek shelter? They accept the angels' message, set out to find the manger, and find there the promised Saviour. But they don't keep what they have experienced for themselves; they pass it on. And above all, they praise and glorify God for everything they have experienced. In this way they become the prototypes of a faith to which people of every class can find access. For it is the poorest of all who are the first to make their way to the manger.

The Response of Faith

"Today a Saviour has been born to you!" That is the Christmas message for the shepherds. The choir of angels responds to it with a hymn of praise which for me expresses again and again the heart of the Christian faith: "Glory to God in the highest heaven, and peace on earth, goodwill towards men"—toward human beings. At this point, and at this point only, I cannot accept the modern alteration to the rendering in Luther's Bible or in the 1611 English text, even though it corresponds more exactly to the biblical wording. The modern version talks about peace on earth "among those whom God favours." This does not merely do away with the wonderful rhythm of the three equal parts. It also encourages a misunderstanding—as if God's peace were only for certain people, the ones whom God favours. But this would be an absolute contradiction of the Christmas message, which is meant for everyone, the poor shepherds in the fields as well as the wise astrologists from the East. So at this point I adhere to the language of my childhood's faith: the glory is God's alone, so peace and righteousness should spread throughout the earth, and all human beings should be permitted to live in accordance with the dignity conferred on them.

God's glory, peace on earth, and the dignity shared alike by all human beings: in this triad—this threefold chord—I can find myself, can find what sustains my life, and what points it in the right direction. I was once invited to act for a day as chief editor for a daily paper, and to be responsible for the Christmas issue. I suggested putting the whole of it under this threefold chord: "Glory to God in the highest—peace on earth—goodwill towards men." I was surprised at all the things that fit together under the breadth of this Christmas triad. It breathes generosity. It combines thanksgiving and magnanimity. It holds God and the world together. It prevents God from being world-less and the world from being god-less. The fact that God becomes human helps us to remain human ourselves—and to become human again and again.

Seeing Still More

The Christmas story in the Gospel of Luke has a limited cast: the holy family, the shepherds, and the angels. But in the Christmas crib tradition other figures have come to be added. Ox and ass stand beside the crib. The three kings bring their gifts.

What have ox and ass to do with the stable—apart from the fact that it is a more appropriate place for them than it is for Mary, Joseph, and the child? It is only since the Middle Ages that oxen and donkeys have belonged to the Christmas scene. A late (8th-century) Gospel text mentions them for the first time as standing round the newly born Jesus, indeed as worshipping him. This suggests the notion that just as the shepherds represent all humanity, these two animals represent all created beings, who also bow down before the Saviour. The choice of ox and donkey was suggested by a biblical quotation, a verse which says that "the ox knows its owner, and the donkey its master's crib" (Isa. 1:3).

The biblical origin of the figures of the three wise men or kings is much more obvious. They originate in the second Christmas story in the New Testament, which we find in Matthew's Gospel. Wise men from the East have seen a heavenly constellation that points to the birth of a king. So they have set out to follow the star. First of all they go to the city where the king resides, and ask about the newly born ruler. They are told that according to the biblical promise "one who is to rule in Israel" shall come from Bethlehem (Micah 5:2). Following this hint, they find the child in the manger, worship him, and present him with gifts of gold, frankincense, and myrrh. But God tells them not to return home by way of Jerusalem, and not to tell Herod anything about the child (Matt. 2:1-12).

This story is clearly a play on the fact that the Saviour's life is endangered, and can only be saved by means of a miracle. Just as Moses, Israel's leader and lawgiver, was persecuted by the Egyptian pharaoh, so the Jewish king Herod is out to kill Jesus. In this way Jesus takes on the features of a new Moses. A star points to him, just as Balaam already sees a star rising in the east out of Israel (Num. 24:15ff.). But the picture of Herod is modeled on Pharaoh. Pharaoh wanted to have all the sons born of Hebrew women killed (Exod. 1:15-22), and in the same way Herod forms the horrible plan of having all the children in Bethlehem killed. In this way he wants to eliminate his possible rival, the newly born, royal child. But Joseph, obeying what he has been told to do in a dream, takes flight beforehand, and flees to Egypt.

This bloodthirsty story of "the massacre of the innocents" in Bethlehem has no basis in any historical event. It can only be interpreted on the basis of this correspondence between Jesus and Moses, and between Herod and Pharaoh.

That is a way of explaining it, but not of justifying it. For the notion that all the children under two years old in the whole Bethlehem region were killed at the command of King Herod (Matt. 2:16) cuts us to the heart, just as does the account of how Abraham was commanded to sacrifice his son Isaac to God (Genesis 22). The fact that Isaac is graciously saved in the end does not diminish our horror that God could give a father any such command. The story only becomes comprehensible if we see it as a way of explaining why human sacrifice was excluded in Israel from the very beginning. The story about the murder of the children in Bethlehem can be understood only if it is taken as an indication of the special position the evangelist gives the child Jesus, who was born in Bethlehem. But in both cases it is a relief to know that stories of this kind, even if they are found in the Bible, can be understood as legends.

We are still left with the question of how the wise men from the East who knew how to interpret the stars turned into kings. As Matthew's Gospel tells us, they brought with them royal gifts: gold, frankincense, and myrrh. One of the psalms in the Old Testament (Psalm 72) already says that fitting gifts are to be offered to the expected royal prince of peace. But it clearly states that these gifts are to be brought by kings. So Christian tradition turned the wise astrologists into kings (their number matching the three gifts) and gave them the names Caspar, Melchior, and Balthasar. Today in Germany, at Epiphany (6 January), children dressed up as these kings go from house to house with carols or poems, and chalk the letters C + M + B on the doorpost or above the door. The letters represent the names of the kings—Caspar, Melchior, and Balthasar—but they also stand for the prayer that Christ may bless the house (= *Christus Mansionem Benedicat*). That is the reason why the cross stands between the three letters. It is a good custom, even if there is nothing in the New Testament about Caspar, Melchior, and Balthasar.

Customs like this show the overwhelming importance of the Christmas miracle for Christian faith. Christmas casts its spell over the whole world. That is why representatives of that world also find a place at the crib: kings and shepherds, oxen and donkeys. But the sculptor Joachim Dunkel went much further. For his wife, he created a crib to which he added new figures every Christmas. My wife and I were once permitted to visit Dunkel and his wife in the room where the crib was set up. It filled the whole room. Tumblers and tricksters, dogs and dromedaries all played a part in it. The whole world was there, gathered round the child in the manger.

5. Experiencing Mercy

Jesus said, "There was a man who had two sons. The younger of them said to his father, 'Father, give me the share of the property that will belong to me.' So he divided his property between them. A few days later the son gathered all that he had and travelled to a distant country, and there he squandered his property in dissolute living. When he had spent everything, a severe famine took place throughout that country, and he began to be in need. So he went and hired himself out to one of the citizens of that country, who sent him to his fields to feed the pigs. He would gladly have filled himself with the pods that the pigs were eating; and no one gave him anything. But when he came to himself he said, 'How many of my father's hired hands have bread enough and to spare, but here I am dying of hunger! I will get up and go to my father, and I will say to him, "Father, I have sinned against heaven and before you; I am no longer worthy to be called your son; treat me like one of your hired hands."' So he set off and went to his father. But while he was still far off, his father saw him and was filled with compassion; he ran and put his arms around him and kissed him. Then the son said to him, 'Father, I have sinned against heaven and before you; I am no longer worthy to be called your son.' But the father said to his slaves, 'Quickly, bring out a robe—the best one—and put it on him; put a ring on his finger and sandals on his feet. And get the fatted calf and kill it, and let us eat and celebrate; for this son of mine was dead and is alive again; he was lost and is found.' And they began to celebrate.

"Now his elder brother was in the field; and when he came and approached the house, he heard music and dancing. He called to one of the slaves and asked what was going on. He replied, 'Your brother has come, and your father has killed the fatted calf, because he has got him back safe and sound.' Then he became angry and refused to go in. His father came out and began to plead with him. But he answered his father, 'Listen! For all these years I have been working like a slave for you, and I have never disobeyed your command; yet you have never given me even a young goat so that I might celebrate with my friends. But when this son of yours came back, who has devoured your property with prostitutes, you killed the fatted calf for him!' Then the father said to him, 'Son, you are always with me, and all that is mine is yours. But we had to celebrate and rejoice, because this brother of yours was dead and has come to life; he was lost and has been found.'"

—Luke 15:11-32

Which Parable?

It begins with the father's compassion. Jesus' mission is to bring this compassion to men and women, and he does so in what he says and in what he does. The Gospels describe this with abundant power. He heals the sick and provides people who are hungry with their daily bread. And in parables he brings out the real point of this commitment.

The most famous of all Jesus' parables is what we know in English as the parable of the prodigal son; in German it is called the parable of the lost son. There are good reasons for giving it this name. In Luke's Gospel it is one of a series of other parables with examples of losing and finding again: a lost sheep and a lost coin (Luke 15:1-10). But for all that, I am talking here about *the parable of the son who is found again.*

Twice the father cries that now the son has been found again. That is the conclusion of the whole parable. Its last sentence reads: "This brother of yours was dead and has come to life, he was lost and has been found." The all-important thing is the fact that the son has been found again and is no longer lost. In what way has he been found again? Through the father's compassion. If it were not for that, we could at most talk about a son who had returned home, but not about a son who had been found again. So if we look at the parable more closely, it does not really centre on the son at all; the centre is the father. It is through the example of the father that Jesus shows us so vividly God's loving commitment to the lost human being.

But this father is not contrasted with only one son. We hear about two. The older one stays at home and helps his father, who is evidently a farmer. The younger one, on the other hand, feels the call of far-off places. He burns all his bridges, with the aim of living his own life just as he likes. So he has the inheritance owed to him paid out, and he takes off.

But his inheritance is soon used up, and he becomes destitute. The only work he can find is the lowest of the low. He can only feed himself from fodder meant for the animals, and even that is denied him. He sees no way out, and is forced to recognize that his foray into the outside world has failed miserably. Then he remembers his father, who employs day labourers on his farm. That seems to him to offer the only way out. So he sets out on the return journey. He makes up his mind to admit his fault to his father, and to renounce his position as son. His audacious hope is that his father will give him work as a day labourer.

Finding Again

The father sees the son coming while he is still a long way off—the son he believed he had lost. He has compassion on him, and hurries to meet him. This movement on the part of the father is decisive. He grasps his son's situation and his heart is touched. Of his own accord he runs to meet the son he had believed he had lost, falls on his son's neck, and kisses him. The father comes to meet the son; it is only after that that the son is able to admit his guilt, as he had intended to do. But his father doesn't react to the confession with words, but in an act, which could not be more symbolic. He has his son splendidly dressed and orders all the preparations to be made for a festive meal. The reason for the feast is clear: "This son of mine was dead and has come to life, he was lost and has been found."

The son came expecting that he would never again be able to assume a son's position. He imagined that the father's utmost concession would be to give him wages and bread as a farm worker. But the father sees his return with the eyes of love, and so he perceives it in a totally different light. He sees his son's return as a turn from death to life, from being lost to being found. And that is reason enough for a great celebration.

Another Brother

The encounter between the father and his younger son is movingly described. But the reaction of the older brother is described equally convincingly. Once again—as between Cain and Abel, and between Abraham and Lot—we are the witnesses to a feud between brothers. Here again the dispute is sparked off by rivalry. But the elder brother doesn't turn to the home-comer, with whom no one had reckoned. He turns to the father, who is actually honouring the dropout with a great welcome party.

We can understand his annoyance. The one brother had escaped from hard work on the family farm in order to enjoy life in the fast lane. He had squandered his inheritance and in doing so had lost his footing, and yet his return is celebrated with a great party. He himself, the elder son, has worked on his father's farm and secured its prosperity. He has fulfilled all his parents' expectations. And yet he has never been given a comparable party. The father replies: "Son, you are always with me and all that is mine is yours. But we had to celebrate and rejoice, because this brother of yours was dead and has come to life; he was lost and has been found."

So the elder brother is supposed to put a brave face on it. Isn't that too much to ask? The surprising turn of the father to the son he thought he had lost is actually accentuated by the apparently matter-of-fact way in which he expects to include the elder brother in his joy. He, too, is supposed to see his brother's return as a turn from death to life. But that admittedly means that he has to rise above himself. When it is a matter of life or death, the rivalry between brothers has to take a back seat. When it is a question of all or nothing, there has to be an end to the adding up of accounts. The older brother is invited to join the celebration and to rejoice over the father's compassion. This compassion does not exclude him; it is there for him as well.

Family Dramas

The younger of the two brothers wants to live his own life. He wants to get over his dependence on other people. So he says goodbye to home and parents, and goes his own way.

This sort of thing is repeated from generation to generation. It is often successful; after a certain time the relationship between parents and children is renewed in a spirit of friendship and love between partners. But in following this path the parents have to learn to let go.

To allow children go their own way is easier said than done. For as a rule parents have clear ideas about the way things should go: education, the choice of a partner, the finding a profession or occupation, then a settled income—everything is supposed to go just as the parents want. The children are to be independent, but at the same time they are supposed to fulfil their parents' expectations. How many tears have been shed when this has failed to happen! But there are sometimes noisy altercations, too; indeed, even denunciations.

Parents and children are inseparable. There is no country in the world where they can be divorced from each other. But that does not rule out deep, indeed fathom-deep, conflicts— on the contrary. A breach can be healed only through reconciliation. Sometimes old wounds heal without many words. What is past is not brought up again. In other cases there are deep and searching discussions. Misunderstandings are cleared away, reproaches are discussed, forgiveness is given and accepted. In both cases, tokens of the reconciliation are important. The surprising offer of a meal together, for example, can signal a new beginning on both sides.

The parable of the son who has been found again can be read as an example of reconciliation in families. It is an encouragement to leave behind misunderstandings in the relationship between parents and children, to face up to the wrong turnings that have been taken, and to make a fresh start together. But in the story there is more still. The encounter between father and son does not just reflect the dynamic in the relationship between the generations. It goes further: it is also a parable for the relationship to God.

Taking Life into One's Own Hands

The parable of the son who has been found again shows us someone who takes his life into his own hands. He wants to decide for himself about the purpose of his life. He wants to be the master of his own future.

We are all familiar with this attitude. Many people view their lives as a possession that they can dispose of as they choose, and the value of which they can determine for themselves. When life loses this value, one simply puts an end to it. Self-determination includes the right to decide the time of one's death.

The well-known photographer Günter Sachs, for example, discovered when he was 78 years old that his speech was slowing down and that there were unexpected gaps in his memory. Having diagnosed for himself that he was suffering from Alzheimer's disease, he drew his own conclusion, and took his own life. Such a step commands respect, even though it should not be declared to be a final exemplary step of liberty.

For simply to snuff life out does not answer the question about life's meaning. In his novel *I'm Not Stiller*, the Swiss writer Max Frisch puts it as follows: "What is on my mind is the fact that it is always the intelligent people who can't wait for death. . . . At the same time I know for sure that it is no use flinging myself into the street, suicide is an illusion . . . a leap without wings . . . into emptiness as the only reality which belongs to me, which can bear me up . . ." (trans. Michael Bullock [London: Methuen, 1958], 71).

We deceive ourselves if we interpret our lives as our possession, and believe that we can plan them just as we like. No one decides the day of his birth, no one chooses his parents. The talents that I develop, the chances that emerge, the conditions under which I lead my life—none of this can be planned. The notion that my life is my own property does not provide me with the clue to reality. The conviction that my life is a gift which God has entrusted to me is much more realistic.

Grace is shown in the tranquility of knowing that I do not have to make my life complete, let alone perfect, in my own strength, for my life always remains a fragment. Falling short and failure, sin, and guilt are a part of even the successful life. The vista into the future opens up if I know that my life is in safekeeping with God. Then I am reached by the father's voice in Jesus' parable: "This son of mine was dead and has come to life; he was lost and has been found."

6. A Challenge for the Individual and for Society

Blessed are the poor in spirit,
for theirs is the kingdom of heaven.
Blessed are those who mourn,
for they will be comforted.
Blessed are the meek,
for they will inherit the earth.
Blessed are those who hunger and thirst for righteousness,
for they will be filled.
Blessed are the merciful,
for they will receive mercy.
Blessed are the pure in heart,
for they will see God.
Blessed are the peacemakers,
for they will be called children of God.
Blessed are those who are persecuted for righteousness' sake,
for theirs is the kingdom of heaven.
—*Matthew 5:3-10*

The Radical Nature of the Sermon on the Mount

It is with the Beatitudes that Jesus' Sermon on the Mount begins. This great discourse sets the tone for the whole of Matthew's Gospel. Opinions are divided about the radical character of the Sermon on the Mount. For some it has provided access to Jesus' message. This was true for the theologian Dietrich Bonhoeffer in his work for the German Resistance, for example, or for the physicist and philosopher Carl Friedrich von Weizsäcker. They have described how encountering the Sermon on the Mount changed their lives. Mahatma Gandhi experienced the same thing, although he was a Hindu, not a Christian. The discovery of Jesus' discourse gave him essential impulses for his path of nonresistance. Other people have played down the importance of the Sermon on the Mount. The German chancellor Otto von Bismarck, for instance, declared that no state could be governed on its basis. In saying that he was no more than following the opinion of leading theologians of his time, for whom nothing was so indisputably true as the fact that the Sermon on the Mount had nothing to do with the way a country should be run, but only with the mindset of individual Christians.

Yet the Sermon on the Mount says nothing about any such division of the world into two separate spheres—on the one hand the political order, on the other the Christian way of thinking. So what conclusions can we draw from it for both personal and political life? The dispute as to whether the spirit of the Sermon on the Mount can make its way into politics has still by no means been settled. But even what this terse and concentrated text has to say about personal life goes far beyond what is customary. It is impossible to maintain that these suggestions are radical only in the political sense, but are easily put into practice in personal life. They demand, for example, that we should neither think ill of other people nor speak ill of them. But not many people are prepared for this abstention. It is not only in its application to politics that the Sermon on the Mount throws up problems. It is impossible to overlook the tension between its precepts and the world we live in as a whole.

Perhaps this tension can be described in the following way. We live in a world that is not yet redeemed. It is not only human actions that give rise to tensions and contradictions; nature, too, is characterized by conflicts and violent processes. Animals lie in wait for each other. Earthquakes and tsunamis lay waste to whole regions, and unless safety measures are undertaken in time, they are the cause of many deaths. Nature follows its own laws, and is anything but tame and inoffensive. And human beings continually so employ their freedom in ways that accentuate conflict. The self-interest and rivalry that the story of Cain and Abel exemplifies still dominate the world. Personal dissensions cut people off from one another. Marriages break down, brothers and sisters become alienated, competition dominates the life we share. There is no country in the world that can afford to dispense with the means of force. Even the Vatican has its Swiss Guard. Violence is by no means under control; it continually prevails. The instruments of force have been modernized. They are now deadlier and more precise, and have come to include weapons of mass destruction with which all life on earth can be snuffed out.

And yet in spite of this tension we sense that truth is on the side of the love which comes to meet us in the Sermon on the Mount. Where love rules, a shared life can succeed. The spirit of forgiveness and renunciation of force make new beginnings possible. We can all think of examples. Love blossoms once again, and broken relationships are healed. Solidarity with our neighbour overcomes frontiers; relief and charitable organizations stand by the victims of hunger and violence. The spirit of the Sermon on the Mount even takes on political form. In Europe, after the murderous violence of the Second World War that Germany had unleashed, a new political beginning was dared in the spirit of forgiveness. Nonviolence was the mark of the peaceful revolution of 1989 in East Germany. In South Africa, after the end of apartheid, truth and reconciliation were linked together.

The Sermon on the Mount has brought a new tone into the world. Its truth continually strikes out new ways forward. But it is a quiet truth. It doesn't merely proclaim the renunciation of force. It also renounces force for its own part. It doesn't overwhelm—it convinces. It doesn't constrain—it inspires.

The History of the Beatitudes

The Sermon on the Mount doesn't begin with demands; it starts with promises. It doesn't heighten the commandments with which human beings see themselves confronted; it holds up the promises from which they can take their bearings. It begins with eight Beatitudes—eight groups of people who are called fortunate. God's evaluation of them is held out to people who are anything but happy.

This comes out particularly clearly in the version of the Beatitudes we find in the Gospel of Luke (Luke 6:20-22).

> *Blessed are you who are poor,*
> *for yours is the kingdom of God.*
> *Blessed are you who are hungry now,*
> *for you will be filled.*

Blessed are you who weep now,
for you will laugh.
Blessed are you when people hate you, and
when they exclude you, revile you, and defame
you on account of the Son of Man.

These Beatitudes are given a quite direct social thrust. They are addressed to the poor, the hungry, and the sad, all of whom can view their situation in a new light. The poor are promised a better world in which there is no more poverty: the kingdom of God. The hungry will have enough to eat. The sad will have a reason to laugh again. Side by side with these people are three groups of those who are excluded and persecuted for Jesus' sake. The Beatitudes do not say how their situation is going to change. It must be enough for them to know: we have not been forsaken by God; we are in safekeeping with God—we are, in fact, blessed.

In Matthew's Gospel, not only is the number of Beatitudes doubled (eight instead of four); their horizon widens out, too. Want in the social, material sense is not the only thing that humiliates men and women; they can also be excluded and marginalized in a different way. They are denied membership in the community of believers, so that they feel "poor in spirit." People who cannot come to terms with the injustice in the world can be hungry, too: they "hunger and thirst for righteousness."

This expansion can also be interpreted as a narrowing down. That has unfortunately often been the case. Read this way, the Sermon on the Mount would have nothing more to do with politics and economics. It would be dealing not with material necessity but only with poverty of spirit—not with political conflicts but only with meekness as an attitude of mind. Then the place of the Sermon on the Mount would no longer be the unredeemed world in which we live but an inner life in which we could contentedly settle down. But there is no need to interpret the expansion to the Beatitudes in such a way that they lose their comprehensive sense. Instead, they can be set against the wide horizon that the eight Beatitudes trace out.

In Matthew's Gospel, the Beatitudes do not just move into view certain situations in life, but a certain attitude to life as well. The four social Beatitudes that we know from the Gospel of Luke are now linked with four Beatitudes that describe a particular attitude toward living.

A Change of Perspective

For this new attitude toward life the Beatitudes choose unusual words. The people who are called blessed are the meek and the merciful, those with pure hearts, and the peacemakers. In Jesus' time this attitude toward life was just as unusual as it is today, especially talk about the "purehearted" and the "peace-makers." The first of these two expressions has never found its way into everyday language, even now. The attitude toward life these words describe is generally dismissed as impracticable. But Jesus brings about a radically new evaluation. He draws attention to the people who do not elbow their way through life, do not pursue their own advantage, do not make their way by force. It is to them that the future belongs. The gentle and considerate will rule the earth; the people who are prepared for love will experience the love of God; the unassuming will encounter God; the peacemakers will be recognized as being God's sons and daughters.

It is an astonishing change of perspective, and an impressive one. To this the poetic form of the Beatitudes contributes.

We can read the passage like a poem consisting of two verses, each of them containing four Beatitudes, and each Beatitude consisting of two clauses. The rhythm of these two clauses remains in our memories: "Blessed are" begins the first, while the second begins with a simple "for." In the first clause a particular group is addressed, in the second their situation, or their attitude, is linked with a promise. These promises are formulated in different ways. It is only in the first and the last that we meet the same turn of phrase: "theirs is the kingdom of heaven."

This phrase therefore provides the framework for the Beatitudes as a whole. Their theme is the promise of God's rule. That links them with Jesus' proclamation and with the whole way he lived. His whole public ministry stands under the heading that the time is fulfilled and that the kingdom of heaven is at hand (Mark 1:15). In this fulfilled time, the light of God's goodness also falls on the people who until then have stood in the shadows: those who are socially unvalued, those discriminated against because of their religious opinions, or persecuted for their political views, as well as those who have resisted force, cared for the earth, and been merciful. The Beatitudes—God's blessings—are this light of God's goodness.

It is a light that shines over two thousand years. The Beatitudes need no explanation; they speak for themselves. No one finds it difficult to apply them to their own experience and to the political circumstances of their own time. So I shall only enter more closely into three examples, and shall look at the blessing to the poor, the blessing to the peacemakers, and the blessing to those who are persecuted because of their faith.

Poverty

In the wistful eyes of the poorest of the poor, hope takes con-crete form. They should not have to humiliate themselves any-more, like the beggars I met in the rich, and yet so poor, city of Teheran. One of them had taken his violin and wandered between the cars waiting at the traffic lights, in the hope that at a few notes from his instrument the car windows would open and he would be given a few Iranian rials. A few kilo-metres further a young women, her head correctly veiled and with her six-month-old child on her arm, looked into a car with her dark, poverty-filled eyes. But they all drove on before any of them had compassion on her. The blessing to the poor reminds us to be aware of the small and unimportant people—and the smallest of all.

In our world, poverty is a mass phenomenon. At the moment the world population is estimated to be seven billion people, and it is growing by seventy-nine million every year. The attempts to diminish hunger and destitution do not keep pace with this increase. In the year 2000, the international community committed itself to halve poverty in the world by 2015. But the realization of this obligation is still very far off.

At present 840 million people are permanently underfed; at the same time 500 million are overfed, to put it politely. Pov-erty is shown nowhere more clearly than in the lack of access to foodstuffs, clean water, and hygienically bearable living conditions. In our world this absolute poverty is linked with growing differences in the standard of living and in living con-ditions. The increasing social contrasts can be found not only in countries in the world's poverty belt or in the newly indus-trialized countries, but in the rich developed countries, too. On the grounds that these countries have to be competitive on the global labour market, the working income is diminishing or stagnating even in wealthy countries, while managerial incomes and investment earnings are rising dramatically.

Developments of this kind are not only reflected in statistics. They emerge above all in personal life, in individual situations. Only a few can escape from poverty through their own efforts. Many people have no chance to give their lives a turn for the better through their own ability. They remain chained to the conditions in which they were born, above all because of malnutrition from early childhood onwards, or because their families had no access to education.

In a situation like this the hunger and thirst for righteousness has a clear thrust: prosperity must be increased not just for the few, but for as many as possible. So high priority must be given to the fight against poverty. The most important way of fighting poverty is to make active participation possible through education. People who allow their efforts to be prompted by the hunger and thirst for righteousness do not act in vain.

Peace

Year after year the earth witnesses a multiplicity of violent conflicts—28 of them in 2010, for example. The victims among the civilian population, and among soldiers, run into the thousands. Peacemakers take very seriously the task of containing daily violence, in small matters and in great. But at the same time they try to find ways of ensuring a shared political life without force.

The term *pacifist* goes back to the blessing promised to the peacemakers, for in the Latin translation of the Beatitudes the peacemakers are called *pacifici*. Luther followed this precisely when he used the German expression *Friedfertige*, by which, as he explicitly stressed, he meant people who "manufacture" peace. So for him peacemaking did not mean a passive attitude; it meant an active intervention for peace. It was only in the 20th century that the word *pacifism* came to be understood exclusively in the sense of a renunciation of force, and no longer as an active responsibility for peace, as the word's literal meaning suggests.

The origin of the pacifism talked about in the Sermon on the Mount points in a distinct direction. What is meant is the task of making an end of violence wherever it rules, and at the same time the task of working for a peaceful life together, wherever that is possible. Dietrich Bonhoeffer had just this kind of pacifism in mind when he said: "The decisive question is not how I can escape my own responsibility through some heroic act, but how a future generation will be able to live." If we follow Bonhoeffer's way of looking at things, what is in line with the spirit of the Sermon on the Mount is an attitude of "responsible pacifism" in which two goals belong together: the surmounting of force, and the link between justice and peace. The preferential option for freedom from force, and the guiding concept of just peace are the basic principles of a Christian peace ethic that takes its bearings from the Sermon on the Mount.

In the United States, the United Church of Christ explicitly identifies itself in its communications as "A Just Peace Church." I still remember how deeply I was impressed by this self-description when I first came across it many years ago. The message it puts across is not, we want *to become* a church for just peace, but we *are* a church of just peace.

There is nothing exciting about this self-identification in itself; it is simply a means of communicating information. And yet I couldn't get this one out of my head. In its everyday correspondence, a church is professing that it stands for peace. It is signaling that peace is not just a subject for ethical responsibility, but more: that this subject is bound up with the life of this church as a whole. For it is a church in which Christ himself makes peace and where Christ gives the courage for peacemaking. So Christian life and action is directed toward peace, not war. Righteousness and war do not belong together, but only righteousness and peace.

There are some verses in one of the psalms that were largely forgotten for a long time but have attracted increased attention in recent years. They talk about the people who hope that "[in our land] steadfast love and faithfulness will meet; righteousness and peace will kiss each other. Faithfulness will spring up from the ground, and righteousness will look down from the sky. The LORD will give what is good, and our land will yield its increase. Righteousness will go before him, and will make a path for his steps" (Ps. 85:9-13). A comparably important passage in the epistle to the Ephesians acknowledges Jesus Christ as the quintessence and pledge of peace: "[Jesus Christ] is our peace; in his flesh he has made both groups into one and has broken down the dividing wall, that is, the hostility between us.... [He has] proclaimed peace to you who were far off and peace to those who were near; for through him both of us have access in one Spirit to the Father" (Eph. 2:13-18).

A Christian peace ethic is certainly characterized by a clear preference for nonviolence; but there are undoubtedly situations in which this preference must not be misused to justify a mere failure to act. Ever since the division of Europe ended in 1989, we have witnessed a return of war on European soil, too. During these years we have seen the political and humanitarian tragedies in Afghanistan and Iraq, in Rwanda and the Sudan, in fragmented Yugoslavia and in the Middle

East. In 2011 dramatic conflicts in North Africa, especially in Libya, were added. In view of these violent events, whether foreign intervention as the ultimate resort could be justified has become a key question in peace ethics. In this context, soldiers and their officers are thinking about killing and being killed in a new way, as well as about the charge to kill and the responsibility for letting themselves be killed. For these people the ethic of the Fifth Commandment is coming pressingly close.

For every thinking person the threshold for the use of force is high. It is only permissible for the state to use its monopoly of force when this serves to prevent or end violence—that is to say, in pursuance of its obligation to protect human beings. In defining this threshold, reflections again surface that can also be found in the century-old tradition of the doctrine about the just war: questions about the grounds for its permissibility, its authorization, its right intention, whether it is the ultimate resort, its proportionality, and finally the distinction between the military and the civilian population. But even when all these criteria seem to be met, it is still impossible to talk about a "just war" or a "justifiable" use of force, since however carefully one thing is weighed up against another, the use of force always involves guilt. In a particular situation, this guilt can seem to be inescapable; but it cannot be viewed as right. If, in a situation that permits no other possibility, a decision is made in favour of the (even then) guilt-laden path of counterforce as the ultimate resort, this does not justify the use of force as such. For that very reason the application of force as the last resort must be strictly subordinated to the rule of law; it must always serve to preserve law or to make a state of law possible.

Because law must be paramount, any action that makes victims of soldiers and civilians without distinction is unacceptable, even during situations of civil war. The German air strike in Kunduz, Afghanistan, on 4 September 2009, in which 142 people, many of them civilians, fell victim, is an example. Anyone who after careful political consideration assents to the use of force must also consider from the outset how this intervention can be ended. For the binding criterion for the action remains the surmounting of force.

Persecution

The early Christians were already harried and persecuted because of their faith. The apostles Peter and Paul repeatedly landed in prison. Many a supporter of Jesus became a victim of the first persecution. This experience is reflected in the blessing promised to the persecuted. God's grace is close to anyone who has to fear for body, life, and liberty because of his or her faith. At a time when religious liberty is respected and protected as a human right, we should like to think that this Beatitude has lost its topical application. But that is unfortunately not the case. In the countries belonging to the Eastern bloc up to 1989, and in China or North Korea, Christians have been, and are still, prevented from freely confessing and practicing their faith. Here discrimination in the sectors of education and professional life has continually proved to be one of the most effective methods of hindering the free practice of religion.

In some Islamic countries today Christians are suffering from massive repression. This can go together with direct danger to life, as shocking examples from Egypt, Iraq, and Nigeria show. Even under a secular constitution such as that in Turkey, the rights of Christians are infringed. The reproach of proselytizing can serve as a pretext for acts of murder. But acts of murder committed out of religious fanaticism are by no means confined to a single country.

Among many of its neighbours, Turkey counts today as a model. The uprisings in Tunisia, Egypt, Syria, or Libya are much more closely oriented toward the Turkish model than toward Western European or North American ideas of democracy that emphasizes human rights. Islam as a part of national identity, economic progress, political moderniza-tion, and clear partisan support for the Palestinians count as the exemplary features of the Turkish political model. Other than in Indonesia, which recognizes the equal rights of six religions, in Turkey and the countries that strive to copy it, non-Muslim groups among the population are at most toler-ated, but do not enjoy equal rights as far as religious liberty is concerned.

And yet Europe's intervention on behalf of the perse-cuted frequently sounds far from convincing. All too often, the export of arms and munitions takes precedence over the protection of human rights. Economic relations continually push into the background the need for intervention on behalf of freedom of religion and belief; the political stance toward China shows this particularly clearly. When it still takes months for 2,500 Christians from Iraq to be admitted to Ger-many, the deficits in credibility remain alarmingly great.

When the persecuted are called blessed, this also involves the obligation to stand by them, and not to abandon them. For Christians, religious liberty as a human right is a central theme. That also means that Christians have a duty to stand up for the religious liberty of people whose beliefs differ from their own. For religious liberty is indivisible.

The blessing for the persecuted touches the very nerve cen-tre of our civilization. This civilization has more to do with

the Sermon on the Mount than people believe, as they maintain its political impracticability. Far from being impracticable, the spirit of the Sermon on the Mount is indispensible, not
only for personal life but for political life, too.

7. At the Centre, the Cross

I believe in Jesus Christ his only Son, our Lord,
who was conceived by the Holy Ghost,
born of the Virgin Mary,
suffered under Pontius Pilate,
was crucified, died and was buried;
he descended into hell.
On the third day he rose again from the dead;
he ascended into heaven,
and sitteth on the right hand of God the Father Almighty;
from thence he shall come to judge the quick and the dead.
—*The Apostles' Creed, 2nd to 4th century CE, Second Article*

Lord, make me an instrument of your peace.
Where there is hatred, let me love;
where there is injury, let me pardon;
where there is conflict, let me reconcile;
where there is error, let me speak truth;
where doubt threatens, let me bring faith;
where there is despair, let me wake hope;
where there is darkness, let me bring light;
where there is sadness, let me bring joy.

Lord, grant that I may not so much seek to be console as to console,
not so much to be understood as to understand,
not so much to be loved as to love.
For it is the one who gives who receives;
it is the one who forgets himself who finds;
it is the one who forgives who is forgiven;
and it is the one who dies who wakens to eternal life.
Amen.
—*Peace prayer attributed to Francis of Assisi, 1181/82–1226*

Become Human—Crucified—Risen

Birth—humiliation—exaltation: through the eyes of Christian faith these are the three steps along the path taken by Jesus Christ. The one who has become human—the one crucified—the one risen: these are the three stages along that path. In all three aspects faith perceives that in Jesus Christ God comes to meet us human beings. In his birth, God shows God's closeness through the very fact that all sovereignty is lacking there. In his death on the cross, God's love shows itself in the sacrifice of the divine life. With Jesus' resurrection from the dead, God makes the total commitment of the crucified Jesus God's own commitment. This death benefits every human being and opens up for them a new access to God.

The early Christians already concentrated their whole attention on this happening. They meditated on it and extolled it in song. They laid such great stress on it that the stories about Jesus' life and the accounts of his preaching sometimes receded into the background. The Apostles' Creed is an obvious example. It jumps from Jesus' birth straight to his sufferings under Pontius Pilate. This does not make Jesus' ministry unimportant. But the three steps—the incarnation, the crucifixion, the resurrection—come to the fore all the more forcibly.

What stands at the centre is the cross. The narrative about Jesus' sufferings and death, with the different emphases given to it in the four different Gospels, continually moves men and women to the depths. Why is Jesus condemned? Why this punishment, with its excessively cruel method of execution, a punishment that, according to Roman law, was imposed only on those convicted of a severe crime? The condemned person had to carry the crossbeam himself as far as the place of crucifixion; then he was nailed or tied to stake and crossbeam. The torment was additionally drawn out until, after unendurable suffering, the victim's heart stopped beating.

"But Jesus cried again with a loud voice and yielded up the ghost." When we hear these words in one of Bach's Passions, or hear them read at a Good Friday service, we catch our breath. The cross comes before us as the place of forsakenness for which no words can be found.

And yet Jesus' cross has astonishing repercussions. This is most clearly brought out in the Gospel of John. It presents this way of the cross as a sequence of encounters (John 19:17-30).

Five Encounters

The cross of Jesus brings people together who would otherwise have had nothing to do with each other.

First of all are the two nameless men who are crucified with him, one on the right hand, the other on the left. What the forgiveness of sins means is made plain by the very place where Jesus dies: he is executed between two criminals. Society wants to be rid of them—Jesus turns to them.

What a contrast: in the next encounter we have to do with the power holders and decision makers—with the Roman governor Pilate and the Jewish high priests. John's Gospel is anxious to lay a considerable share of the responsibility for Jesus' death on the shoulders of the Jewish spokesmen. But it was not they but only the Roman occupying power that was able to pass such a death sentence and to carry it out.

Beneath Jesus' cross the political power holders and the religious representatives fall foul of each other. They dispute about the right to define the significance of what is happening. Pilate wants the words "The King of the Jews" to be put up over the cross. A placard of this kind was supposed to state the reason why a person was put to death on the cross. No, the high priests counter: the notice should read that "This man said I am King of the Jews." At all events, a claim to political power is put forward as reason for the death penalty— although according to John's Gospel Jesus explicitly declared before Pilate that his kingdom was not of this world.

The third encounter is very different. There are soldiers sitting below the cross. They are watching to see that the execution is correctly carried out. Even while the victim is still alive, they already turn their attention to what he leaves behind him. As fortuitously as they themselves are thrown together, they throw dice for the possession of a piece of clothing belonging to the condemned man. The clothes are cut up and divided, and lots are drawn for the tunic. They don't know that by doing this they are fulfilling the Scriptures: "They divide my clothes among themselves, and for my clothing they cast lots" (Ps. 22:18).

The fourth encounter is the most personal of all. In the moment of farewell under the cross, a new relationship comes into being. Looking down from the cross, Jesus brings his mother and his favourite disciple together. In the hour when they say goodbye to him, they are joined together: adoptive mother and adopted son, as it were: "Woman, here is your son," and to the disciple, "Here is your mother."

Jesus dies, and this death sets love free. Beneath the cross, in the midst of outer and inner darkness, not only are hopes and dreams shattered, but a new love begins as well. Not only a farewell, but a new beginning, too: God reconciles Godself with the world, and that radiates out into the relations between human beings. The cross moves into the light of a hope that does not divide people but brings them together.

How far this is from the way the cross has been used in later times! How far from the sign of victory that the emperor Constantine saw in a dream before the decisive battle for Rome, accompanied by the promise, "In this sign you will conquer"—how far from the cross that became the emblem of the crusades. Today, for some people the cross is no more than a decorative object without any meaning for them, while in Germany other people object to being taught in schoolrooms where there is a cross on the wall. How far such conflicts are from the cross as a sign of hope that does not divide but join!

The final encounter goes even further. "It is finished." Those were Jesus' last words on the cross. Here his path is completed. The loneliness of the cross leads on to fellowship with God. What seems to the world in general to be a humiliation is for believers an exaltation. The one who suffers so wretchedly is in his suffering very close to God. In his helplessness God's power itself is displayed: love. "No one has greater love than this, to lay down one's life for one's friends," we read in the same Gospel (John 15:13).

Just as he did in his lifetime, even in his death on the cross Jesus also lets new relationships come into being between human beings. But above all he establishes a new relationship to God. In the ultimate forsakenness of the cross, God comes close to us: "In Christ God was reconciling the world to himself, not counting their trespasses against them, and entrusting the message of reconciliation to us" (2 Cor. 5:19). On the cross this path was painfully completed: "It is finished."

In these very words we hear that Jesus is inseparably bound up with God. This bond is endorsed when the raising to the cross is followed by the raising to God. This is what the accounts of Jesus' resurrection and ascension tell us. Their essential content does not depend on the concepts which are used to emphasize that Jesus did not remain in death. What is central for these stories is the certainty that God holds unswervingly to Jesus, and that God's message continues and endures. The message of God's forgiving love is the message for all human beings.

The Suffering God

God takes the suffering on Godself. This stands in the greatest possible tension with the usual pictures people have of God. God is the one than whom nothing greater can be thought: at an earlier point with this tenet, I cited the medieval theologian Anselm of Canterbury. When the Christian creed calls God the Almighty it is saying nothing different. In Christian history the acknowledgment of the Almighty Creator has frequently been associated with a picture of God that originally derives from Greek notions about the gods: God assumes the features of Zeus, the father of the gods, and is pictured as an old man with a beard.

But for the Christian faith, when God is associated with a human face, that has a wholly different meaning. God's kindness toward human beings is shown in the person of Jesus Christ. God takes human form and follows the path of suffering. It is in suffering that God displays God's almighty power. It is in divine love that God reveals God's greatness. This has nothing to do with the idea of an "impassable God," a God incapable of suffering, a concept that was maintained for so long.

The wording of the creed itself can save us from any such idea. It says nothing about Jesus' life, ministry, and preaching. But it explicitly stresses the suffering of the Son of God: "Suffered under Pontius Pilate." No biblical scene shows this more impressively than Jesus' wrestling with his fate in the garden of Gethsemane, shortly before the Roman soldiers seize him, and his trial begins.

In the loneliness of the garden Jesus prays: "My Father, if it is possible, let this cup pass from me; yet not what I want but what you want." Faced with this struggle, he seeks the nearness of his disciples; but they are asleep. Dumbfounded, he asks them: "Could you not stay awake with me one hour?" (Matt. 26:39f.).

With his plea to the Father and his question to the disciples, something extraordinary begins: it is the beginning of God's messianic suffering in the world. The disciples are asked to participate in this suffering—at least for an hour. This simple request tells us a great deal both about God and about the place of Christians in the world. God turns to the world without reservation; God involves Godself in it to the point of the most profound suffering. Christians are asked to share in this suffering of God's in the world; so the world is the place of Christian faith. God's commitment to the world and faith's responsibility for the world belong indissolubly together.

The decisive turn in Jesus' struggle in the garden of Gethsemane comes about because ultimately he does not rely on what he himself wants; he trusts himself to God. So he begs God to let the cup of suffering pass him by, but adds: "Not what I want but what you want." Trust in God shows itself in the preparedness to hold fast to God's will in seemingly hopeless situations.

But that does not mean subjecting oneself to evil—on the contrary. Those who hold fast to God's will develop not just the readiness to surrender to what cannot be changed but also the power to resist. They trust that the necessary strength will be given them. This strength is not a secure possession; it is not founded on self-confidence. In it God's Spirit shows itself, which means that the trust is also trust in the Spirit.

This Spirit also gives us the strength to admit our own faults and mistakes. They weigh heavily. But they do not have the final word. God can make good come even out of faults and mistakes. It may even be, in certain circumstances, that these things are no less valuable than what we consider to be our own best achievements.

The accounts of the passion in the New Testament do not conceal Jesus' fear in the garden of Gethsemane and on the cross: "My God, my God, why have you forsaken me?" he cries on the cross (Matt. 27:46). But in spite of this cry he remains close to God and commends his spirit into his Father's hands. Just because of that, Christians can affirm that in the crucified Christ God also suffers. And just because of that, they can know that in their own suffering they are in God's safe keeping.

Following Jesus

In Christian history the preparedness for suffering and poverty have always counted as the signs of a consistent discipleship of Jesus. The readiness to take suffering and deprivation on oneself, to renounce all prosperity for the sake of one's neighbour—indeed, even to live without a family of one's own—all this brings out the total and unreserved commitment to Jesus.

The very way Jesus' disciples lived already makes this evident. They have been called "wandering radicals"; they renounced a home of their own and turned to sympathizers who gave them a roof over their heads. In Jesus' pronouncements on discipleship, receiving his disciples is explicitly said to be the same as receiving Jesus. But the person who receives Jesus receives God also. In this way what the "sympathizers" do is undoubtedly honoured; yet at the same time the way of the cross is described in seemingly harsh words as the only way of discipleship: "Whoever loves father or mother more than me is not worthy of me; and whoever loves son or daughter more than me is not worthy of me; and whoever does not take up the cross and follow me is not worthy of me." This narrow path is stressed in such uncompromising terms because it is on that path that the real meaning of life is to be found: "Those who find their life will lose it, and those who lose their life for my sake will find it" (Matt. 10:37-39).

So even in the biblical accounts themselves two forms of the life of faith are distinguished; the way taken by the "wandering radicals," and the way of the "sympathizers." The first are promised that they will find their life by losing it; the others are promised that when they support those who follow Jesus they will receive Jesus himself.

The difference between these two ways of living has had great importance throughout Christian history. The retreat from the world—and participation in worldly life; communal forms of living—and participation in the world's doings and dealings; the renunciation of all possessions—and the increasing of prosperity; celibacy—and the founding of a family—we meet these two basic forms of Christian existence again and again. The models especially held up are the people who devote themselves entirely to the discipleship of Jesus and renounce everything that distracts them from this commitment. They act as models even for those who do not decide for so radical a way of living but who are "sympathizers" of Jesus, rather than "disciples."

Discipleship means following the way of the cross. This becomes symbolically clear from the example of Francis of Assisi. All at once the marks of Jesus' suffering appeared on his body—the first case of a "stigmatization" of this kind of which we are told. This was a sign that his whole life was directed toward the discipleship of the crucified Jesus; Francis also interpreted his illnesses during his final years as a sign of his following of the cross.

In his case the new way of living required a radical conversion. For Francis came from a wealthy merchant's family. But his conversion went hand in hand with the renunciation of a profession and a settled, middle-class life; as an itinerant preacher he lived in complete poverty and devoted himself to the care of lepers. Soon others joined him; they also committed themselves to a life of poverty and penance, devoted to men and women and the church. From this the traditions of the mendicant orders and what is known as the poverty movement began. Again and again, the radical character of the Franciscans proved to be an impulse for the renewal of the church and of faith.

The same impulse emerges in the "peace prayer" that is ascribed to Francis of Assisi. True, this is not one of the texts that he himself left behind, but it breathes his spirit: the spirit of self-giving and neighbourly love, of forgiveness and a new beginning, of selflessness and care for others. The person who prays the prayer is led into a devotion marked by faith, hope, and love.

This prayer has become a fundamental text for a Christian way of life that sees faith in Jesus Christ as involving the obligation to work for justice, peace, and the preservation of creation. This orientation has put a profound stamp on ecumenical Christianity in recent years, and for many people it has opened up a new approach to Christian faith. It has done much to help Christians in Eastern and Western Europe, as well as in East and West Germany, to grow together. The "conciliar process" (as this movement has also been called) has helped essentially to promote the intervention of Christian groups and churches on behalf of human and civil rights, encouraging them to take their responsibility for peace seriously; and in this way it has helped to overcome the divisions in Germany and Europe. The contribution of the churches to the peaceful revolution of 1989 in East Germany took form in the prayers for peace held during those years. It grew out of the spirit that finds expression in Francis of Assisi's peace prayer.

8. Freedom and Responsibility

A Christian is a free lord over all things and subject to none.
A Christian is a dutiful servant of all things and subject to everyone.

From all this it must be concluded that a Christian does not live in himself but in Christ and in his neighbour, in Christ through faith, in his neighbour through love. Through faith he is carried beyond himself into God; from God he is carried back to himself through love, and yet always abides in God and in divine love, as Christ says (John 1:51): "Hereafter ye shall see heaven open and the angels of God ascending and descending upon the Son of man."
—*Martin Luther, "The Freedom of a Christian," 1520*

Just as Jesus Christ is God's assurance of the forgiveness of all our sins, so and with same earnestness he is also God's powerful claim upon our whole life; through him we experience a joyful deliverance from the godless ties of this world for a free, grateful service towards those he has created.
—*Barmen Theological Declaration, 1932, Thesis 2*

Responsibility before God and Human Beings

In a New York prison a chaplain is visiting a young man who has killed his mother. Full of understanding sympathy, the pastor talks to the prisoner. He reminds him of his father's alcohol addiction, and of the district he came from, where violence was commonplace, and the people living there were degraded by poverty. He tells the young man soothingly that it was not he who committed the act; it was the evil conditions. But then the young man suddenly shouts at him: "No! It was *I* who killed my mother, not the conditions!"

Over against an understanding pastor, a murderer insists that he is the author of his own act. He doesn't want his own responsibility to be taken from him: he stands by his guilt. He insists on the dignity of being the determining subject of his own life. He insists on his own freedom, even if it is a freedom he has misused. For freedom is in the first place the sense of having set in motion particular developments just by oneself, and therefore of being responsible for them.

Freedom shows how seriously God takes us human beings. God has given every man and woman an uninfringeable dignity. But God also makes a claim on every one of us. Everyone has to answer for his or her life before God and before other human beings.

Not one of us will live up to this responsibility solely by ourselves. However much we set forth in the world, before God we do not put our lives in order just by our own efforts. It is only thanks to God's grace that we can stand before God. That is true for everyone, not just for a murderer. It was this insight that five hundred years ago led to the Reformation.

Free Out of Grace—Free for Our Fellow Human Beings

Erich Till's film, *Luther*, is well worth seeing. One scene in it brings out this Reformation insight on human dignity very well. The young monk Luther takes the funeral of a suicide, and preaches to a fear-ridden congregation of gravediggers and chance listeners about God's endless compassion, which exceeds all our worldly judgments. This brief scene gives vivid form to the essential Reformation breakthrough, which became the mainspring for the move into modern times. God has given every human being a dignity that is as undeserved as it is uninfringeable. Every individual is addressed by God through his or her conscience, and is answerable to God. That also gives the individual a unique position in society, for no one has power over the individual conscience.

The discovery of the free conscience is the contribution the Christian faith has made to the modern understanding of what "person" means. A moment Till's movie particularly emphasizes is Martin Luther's appearance before the Reichstag in Worms, where he refused to retract his reformative theses, declaring at the end: "Here I stand, I can do no other. God help me. Amen."

But Luther's treatise "On the Freedom of a Christian" can equally well be cited. Its renowned double thesis declares in its first part that the Christian is "a free lord over all things and subject to none." A completely new rank is ascribed to the human being for the very reason that human dignity is rooted not in one's own self but in one's relationship to God. A person's dignity does not depend on one's achievements, place in society, origin, race, or nation but solely on God's recognition of the person. Through God's generosity, every human being enjoys the same dignity. Every person who was imprisoned by the Nazis in a concentration camp and was put to death in the gas chambers: a human being of uninfringeable dignity! In refugee camps in the Sudan, too, or in the Libyan civil war: every person is free, in the freedom conferred by God! These people have no need to subject themselves to anyone: no power in this world has the right to humiliate them.

The results of disregarding this equal dignity of every human being can be seen in the world today, faced as it is by dictatorships, terrorist scares, or personal humiliation. But the 20th century already made plain the need for human dignity in an incomparably cruel way when it experienced its antithesis: the violent and massive infringement of that dignity. That is why human dignity and human rights were put at the centre of the new political beginning after 1945, at the end of the Second World War. The Universal Declaration of Human Rights of 10 December 1948 was a milestone in this development. The declaration did not acknowledge the Christian roots of human rights as having precedence over other reasons. But the Christian view of the human being undoubtedly provides a powerful motivation for maintaining the universal validity of human rights.

The Christian image of human beings sees human dignity as a gift entrusted to them. We live from the dignity given to us; we do not manufacture it for ourselves. A dignity of this kind can truly be termed "uninfringeable," and the human rights based on it can indeed be called, with the German Constitution, "inviolable" and "inalienable." Freedom of conscience and the courage to believe are anchored in this uninfringeable human dignity. For this, Luther's appearance before the Reichstag in Worms in 1521 is an inspiring symbol as, before emperor and empire, he stood up for the free perception of faith according to one's own knowledge and belief.

The Protestant form of the Christian faith does not accept the notion of religious "achievements" or "works." That in no way means a depreciation of the positive value given to achievements as such, but there the yardstick is a standard obtaining between human beings, not a religious one. How far does what you do benefit your fellow human beings? That is the decisive question. That is why in the second part of his double thesis Luther calls the Christian "a dutiful servant subject to everyone." The abilities and potentialities that have been entrusted to me are supposed to benefit my fellow human beings.

The gifts that I bring with me into the world, the environment in which I grow up, the chances I am offered—none of these things spring from my own achievements but are a gift given me. So the fact that such gifts are unevenly distributed is not a reason for one person to look down on another. Pride over being the architect of one's own fortune needs, and has, a counterbalance: gratitude for the gifts for which I have to thank not myself but God. In using my freedom, the essential point is to deal responsibly with the gifts that have been entrusted to me.

Jubilation and Realism

The freedom of a Christian includes the insight that my own ego is not the centre of the world. It is God's glory, not my own, that sheds the proper light on my ego. So in this light, trouble, darkness, whatever is unfathomable and evil itself do not have the last word. The person who is assured of that can promise and pass this on as a sustaining certainty to the oppressed, weeping, despairing people whom he or she meets.

One of the special things about Luther was that he did not brush aside the riddles and hopelessness of life. The freedom he taught includes the preparedness to bear temptations and assaults on the soul. Here his gaze at the suffering Jesus helped him to endure the hiddenness of God, instead of whitewashing it or drowning it out. Every believer comes up against this hiddenness of God. Everyone experiences the incomprehensible, which cannot be explained but can only be accepted from God's hand. Because God has taken the suffering on Godself we can turn to God with our painful experiences, too. This is not to play down the hard things that happen to us; the protest against them still has its place. But because for Christian faith the cross stands at the centre, Christians can look beyond suffering and pain.

Over against the modern optimistic faith in progress, this is an important counterweight. The triumphal assurance of modern science has fed the notion that it is only a question of time before suffering and pain are completely conquered. But however much the successes of modern medicine command our admiration, they do not eliminate the finitude of human life. Even if physical pain can be alleviated, no medicine in the world can do away with the pain that human beings inflict on each other. Today we are still dependent on a sober picture of the human being, which includes the reality of sin and death.

Luther praised the freedom conferred through faith so highly because he was convinced that left to themselves human beings continually fall into bondage. They find themselves in the clutches of sin and become fixed on themselves. That was why he could call men and women warped beings. But he trusted that through Christ we can escape from this deformation, and can stand up straight and be liberated from the wrong directions our lives have taken. Even as believers, we still live in a conflicting world, but we are no longer imprisoned in sin and death. Yet the loosing of these fetters is not a matter of course, which is the reason Luther appealed so emphatically for a life lived out of freedom.

"We are beggars, that is true." Those are the words, spoken on his deathbed, that Luther left behind. He was exceedingly down-to-earth about himself, too. It is only when we take this lack of illusion into account that we see Luther's double thesis, with its jubilant tone, in the depth it requires: "A Christian is a free lord over all things and subject to none. A Christian is a dutiful servant of all things and subject to everyone."

Conflict and Standing the Test

The conjunction of self-confident freedom and selfless intervention on behalf of other people lies at the heart of Protestant convictions. In this conjunction Christian faith emerges as an attitude to life that points further than the philosophy which is sometimes also put forward as freedom: concentration on one's own advantage, combined with indifference toward the way other people have to live. A narrowly egoistical interpretation of freedom of this kind is practiced not only by individuals. It can also become the dominant motivation in economic life, as we can see from excesses on the financial markets, or from the one-sided orientation toward shareholders' profits, the so-called shareholder value. We even come across a similar attitude in the church; it is especially appalling when individuals misuse its charitable services—that is, the church's helping hands—for their own advantage. The provision of a Maserati as a church's "company car" is a particularly disgusting example.

A contracted view determined by egoism can also become a political doctrine. Then it is solely the interests of one's own country that determine policy. The point can even be reached when the conviction about the superiority of one's own ideology, or one's own race, sweeps away respect for the equal dignity of all human beings. The ideological excesses and unrestrained acts of violence committed under the National Socialist regime in Germany showed this in a terrifying way. At the beginning, enthusiasm steamrolled all doubts. "The new national awakening" was exuberantly hailed. The shadow side was ignored. The hope for an economic boom was stronger than the sense of responsibility for the equal rights of everyone. Many Christians let themselves be seduced when the national "nomos" or "law of life" was proclaimed, and the Jews were made the scapegoats for everything that had gone wrong.

Contradicting that seductive doctrine openly was the great service rendered by the Confessing Church. In the era of National Socialism its members were a minority in Protestantism; but it held high a sign of hope that pointed beyond the dark days of Hitler's rule. With the Theological Declaration passed in 1934 by a confessional synod held in Barmen (now part of Wuppertal), it gave an expression to Protestant liberty that had a far-wider influence than its authors could have guessed at the time. For example, when decades later resistance against apartheid in South Africa sought for a convincing voice, it found an orientation in the Barmen Theological Declaration.

The note of freedom in this declaration has always impressed me. At a time when godless power was about to exert its rule over men and women, the declaration proclaimed "a joyful liberation from the godless ties of this world for free, grateful service to those God has created." It contradicted all the ideas which claimed that political life was subject to its own laws. It certainly realistically recognized that the threat of force also has a part to play in a country's actions, if right and peace cannot be secured in any other way. But force had to be subject to the rule of law, and the state was committed to the task of ensuring freedom: for the authors of the declaration this was unquestionable. The fact that in both respects the National Socialist state pursued the precisely opposite path was already obvious in 1934 to those with eyes to see; others noticed it only when it was too late. Nevertheless, it remains a powerful sign of hope that Protestant Christians perceived that Christian liberty provides the standard and the driving power for the necessary resistance. Some of these people took the risky step into active resistance, and their legacy still has an enduring influence.

"From the liberation from the godless ties of this world for free, grateful service to those God has created." That is how the Barmen Theological Declaration described a movement that is still necessary even under democratic conditions. For democracy itself does not protect any of us from delivering ourselves up to the "godless ties of this world." Standards have gone awry, for example, when the claims of people living today determine everything and the exploitation of nature is knowingly continued at the cost of future generations. But standards have also become distorted, too, when money is turned into a god, so that an increase in profits is made the sole purpose of economic activity. In cases of this kind, too, we need a liberation from the godless ties of this world for free, grateful service to those God has created.

A Christian attitude to life helps us to keep in view the well-being of others as well as our own. This balance is more easily achieved if we have learned to look beyond ourselves to the God who confers life and liberty.

9. Signposts of Freedom

1. I am the Lord your God, you shall have no other gods beside me.
2. You shall not take the name of the Lord your God in vain.
3. Remember the Sabbath day, to keep it holy.
4. Honour your father and mother.
5. You shall not kill.
6. You shall not commit adultery.
7. You shall not steal.
8. You shall not bear false witness against your neighbour.
9. You shall not covet your neighbour's house.
10. You shall not covet your neighbour's wife, or his manservant, or his maidservant, or his cattle, or anything that is his.
   —*The Ten Commandments, in Martin Luther's Small Catechism,*
      1529/1531

Then God spoke all these words:

I am the LORD your God, who brought you out of the land of Egypt, out of the house of slavery; you shall have no other gods before me.

You shall not make for yourself an idol, whether in the form of anything that is in heaven above, or that is on the earth beneath, or that is in the water under the earth. You shall not bow down to them or worship them; for I the LORD your God am a jealous God, punishing children for the iniquity of parents, to the third and the fourth generation of those who reject me, but showing steadfast love to the thousandth generation of those who love me and keep my commandments.

You shall not make wrongful use of the name of the LORD your God, for the LORD will not acquit anyone who misuses his name.

Remember the sabbath day, and keep it holy. Six days you shall labour and do all your work. But the seventh day is a sabbath to the LORD your God; you shall not do any work—you, your son or your daughter, your male or female slave, your livestock, or the alien resident in your towns. For in six days the LORD made heaven and earth, the sea, and all that is in them, but rested the seventh day; therefore the LORD blessed the sabbath day and consecrated it.

Honour your father and your mother, so that your days may be long in the land that the LORD your God is giving you.

You shall not murder.

You shall not commit adultery.

You shall not steal.

You shall not bear false witness against your neighbour.

You shall not covet your neighbour's house; you shall not covet your neighbour's wife, or male or female slave, or ox, or donkey, or anything that belongs to your neighbour.

—*Exodus 20:1-17*

Forgotten

A telephone call to a bishop's office. It was even the bishop himself who answered. A journalist was on the line: a mention of the Ten Commandments had suddenly cropped up in the editorial office, but no one knew quite exactly what they were. Everyone stumbled over them. Where could they actually be found, he asked, and how could one get hold of the text?

The bishop came to the rescue. After a few minutes a fax with the Ten Commandments was in the editor's office. In order to make it easier for the journalists, he sent them the short version of the Commandments that Martin Luther had included in his Small Catechism, for this catechism was supposed to present the substance of Christian doctrine in "brief, plain and simple" form. Luther's Ten Commandments fit onto a single page. The version in the book of Exodus needs rather more space.

Whether short or long, for many people the content of the Ten Commandments is vague and cloudy. Until even a few generations ago, they were familiar to most people. But today they have become largely unknown. To grow up with them is no longer a matter of course. For a long time learning by heart was regarded as antiquated, and now even Luther's short version is no help.

But the fact that the Ten Commandments, like other key biblical texts, have ceased to be familiar to everyone, also offers a chance. We can grapple with them afresh. Admittedly, in order to do this one must often begin at ground zero, and this takes courage. But it is also enjoyable to respond to children's curiosity when they want to know: What are the Ten Commandments, and how can they be put into practice? Courage and curiosity—these are incidentally two virtues that traditionally have not been highly regarded, but which ought now to be brought back into favour. For they can help us not to stop short at breaking with traditions but to go on to establish new ones instead.

The chances for this are favourable. We are experiencing a new concern to find reliable norms. Many people are on the search for meaning and a secure foothold. We can be glad, indeed proud, when we find new space for the forgotten texts, for the sayings that have been rejected and the images that have been driven out.

The Eleventh Commandment

The German Protestant TV talk show *Tacheles* (i.e., "Speaking Frankly") devoted a series of programs to the Ten Commandments. In this series young people were asked which commandment was the most important for them. Frequent answers were "You shall not kill" and "Honour your father and mother." They were also asked what commandment ought to be added. They replied: "You shall respect children" or "You shall preserve the environment for those who come after you." When the agnostic Thea Dorn was asked about an Eleventh Commandment, she gave the striking answer: "You shall not waste your life." Less serious but also worth thinking about was the reply of the now-late poet Robert Gernhardt: "You shall not make a lot of noise." The best-known proposal for an Eleventh Commandment is undoubtedly the simple advice: "You shall not let yourself be caught."

Hardly anyone notices, incidentally, that the Ten Commandments do not begin with any of the demands that are so often cited. They don't begin with a command at all. Their first sentence reads: " I am the LORD your God, who brought you out of the land of Egypt, out of the house of slavery." This self-introduction of God's is remarkable in itself. What stands at the beginning is the reminder of God's saving act. Everything begins with the deliverance from slavery. God comes to meet us in what God does. God is not just a fixed, unchangeable entity. God cannot be instrumentalized. God has no address and no telephone number we can simply store on our mobiles. But I can turn to God in prayer, talk to God as Father, address God as an intimate friend.

Free from False Gods

"I am the LORD your God." God's self-introduction is where the Ten Commandments begin. It is only after this that the first demand follows, the First Commandment: "You shall have no gods before me." Just as too little importance is attached to the introduction—the assurance of freedom—the same can be said of the First Commandment—the signpost pointing to freedom. And yet its topical force can hardly be overestimated. The freedom of faith proves itself in freedom from false gods. How do we know that they are false? Because they enslave people, rob them of their freedom, make them dependent.

But if God leads us to freedom, God's freedom, too, must also be respected. But this is disregarded if we press God into an image, and worship that image instead of the living God. That is why the Ten Commandments insist on there being no images of God. It is impossible to make a "profile" of God. No proofs of God's existence can approach God's own self. It is not only visual art that falls short. Human reason is also asking too much of itself if it tries to construct an intellectual "mugshot" of God.

As well as the attempt to banish God into a picture of the divine, there is also the false use of God's name. Even through the way they speak, human beings try to have God at their own disposal. "Thank God!" says even the atheist. "Oh, for God's sake!" is a frequent impatient cry. Or: "O God, not that fellow again!" Or: "Then just get on with it, for God's sake!" In the First World War, German soldiers had a buckle on their belts with the inscription "God with us," as if God were a national god who could be brought into position against the enemy. There are many different ways of using God's name for one's own purposes.

When Moses asks God what the divine name is, God answers him out of the burning bush: "I am who I am" or "I will be who I will be" (Exod. 3:14). For Jewish faith, this divine self-introduction is encapsulated in the four letters YHWH. The Jews deduce from the story of the burning bush, as well as from the commandment not to misuse God's name, that there is a prohibition against using the name of God at all. So wherever these four letters appear (the so-called Tetragrammaton), the Jews say: "the LORD" (*Adonai*). For Christians, not every utterance of the divine name is in itself a misuse; it is, rather, a question of whether when we use God's name, God is reverenced.

God as the only God, the image of God, and the name of God—with these three themes the beginning of the Ten Commandments concentrates complete attention on the question about God. For this is an elemental subject. In one way or another, everyone has to grapple with the question: In what do you see the ultimate, all-determining reality? "That on which your heart depends, that is your God": that is the way Martin Luther defined the question about God. Even people who deny God look for a firm foundation for their lives. For some people it is science, for others money, or the things they can buy with money. The Ten Commandments do not just begin with prohibitions—the prohibition against having other gods, the prohibition against pressing God into some picture of the divine, the prohibition against the misuse of God's name. It is rather that this beginning immediately encapsulates the demand to clear away the accumulated rubbish of our own religious or semi-religious ideas and to examine the question: On what does my heart depend?

Part of this religious clearing-up process means leaving behind the all-too-simple pictures of God that are passed down from one generation to another. The pictures of an old man with a beard living up in the clouds are not biblical; they are pagan.

The biblical tradition is quite different. The invisible God of the people of Israel cannot be pictured. It is inconceivable that we could ever fit God into a picture frame. The things that God does reveal themselves as salvation and blessing.

Let us think for a moment of the dramatic scene in which the people of Israel, through Moses's mediation, receive the Ten Commandments. The Israelites have been led out of the land of slavery. Their newly born children are no longer put to death. The forced labour they have endured in the foreign country is at an end. They are not yet in the land of liberty, but they are on the way there. On Mount Sinai God proposes to the people to enter into a covenant with them. The people themselves are to be God's sanctuary. And YHWH will be their mighty God. The Ten Commandments, written with God's finger on the stone tablets, are to serve the preservation of freedom.

We can transfer the events of the Reed Sea and Sinai to the foundational fact in the Christian perception of God. In correspondence with the First Commandment, this could be summed up as follows: "I am the LORD your God. I have exposed myself to the uttermost humiliation and the most profound suffering for you in Jesus Christ, in order to liberate you from the slavery of meaninglessness and guilt. You shall have no other gods beside me."

For Christians, the experience of God comes together in an unsurpassable way in Jesus Christ. In the face of Jesus, God lets Godself be known. The search for an image of God finds an end. God reveals Godself in a human being; this human being is the image of God.

When I open myself for an encounter with God, I see before me the gift of freedom as a wide horizon. When I give glory to the invisible God, I am preserving myself from expecting salvation from false powers.

The main problem in human history are the false gods to which human beings surrender themselves, the gods that they worship, to which they sacrifice everything they have, and sometimes even their own children—the false gods with which force is justified and injustice is reinforced.

Idols always demand sacrifices. Either one sacrifices oneself to them, or one sacrifices other people. So when after a war there is a confession of guilt, people may say, as they did in the Stuttgart Confession of Guilt, drawn up by the Protestant churches in Germany in 1945: "We have believed too little and loved too little." That is true. But the accusation could also be: we believed too much, much too much. People depended, and still depend, on false gods: one's own nation, one's own class, one's own economic advantage. Faith in God teaches us to distrust the nets and snares spread for us by the idols, the monsters that compel us to throw ourselves or our children into their jaws. Our hearts are too precious for them to be dependent on anything except the living God.

We human beings are evidently always in danger of submitting ourselves to gods of this kind. The gods of success, the gods of self-fulfilment, the gods of autonomy, the gods that incline us to let economic criteria rule over all and everything (for example, over Sunday, too), the idolization of maximum profits—all these things show the kind of idolatry that we have to come to terms with today. To retain a sense of proportion even in eras of globalization is by no means a matter of course.

Preserving Freedom

The person who holds fast to Jesus Christ and trusts in God is called to freedom. I look up to the one God and in doing so gain the courage to walk with head held high, and my life acquires a human moderation. The Ten Commandments describe a way pursued in the liberty of faith; they are a Magna Carta for the preservation of liberty. To put it in the words of Psalm 23: "He leads me in right paths for his name's sake."

"You shall . . . you shall not . . ." Because of the way they are worded, the Ten Commandments sound like a restriction, indeed, even like a hindrance, to life's possibilities. They have continually been understood in this sense; human self-determination is to be stifled, limits are to be set to the development of human powers. But the Ten Commandments aim at something different. They want to protect and increase human liberty and dignity. The Ten Commandments are a signpost to freedom. Today, too, they help us to preserve the freedom with which we have been entrusted.

In the commandments that are concentrated on the relationship of human beings to God, this freedom is initially described more precisely as lying in two directions: the one is the relationship to time, the other the mutual relationship of the generations. The commandment about the Sabbath and the commandment about parents are the only two commandments that are formulated in positive terms. They do not forbid, like all the others, but point a path to be followed. They say what we should do, not what we shouldn't.

In the rhythm of the week, the Bible emphasizes one day as a symbol—indeed, a guarantee—of freedom: that is the Sabbath, the day of rest from work. The collective interruption of work is esteemed so highly that it is to be shared not only by human beings but by animals, too. This day is so important that even God's work of creation is directed toward it. The six days of work, the symbol in which the event of creation is summed up, find their conclusion in a day of rest. There is therefore good reason for describing this day of rest, and not human beings, as the crown of creation. In Christendom this day of rest was put together with the Sunday, the day of Jesus' resurrection from the dead. The day when there is a general interruption of work was fused with the day of worship. The freedom from work was joined with the freedom for faith.

Although since that early time living conditions have changed very greatly, the rhythm of the seven-day week has been kept. Both during the French Revolution of 1789 and in the Bolshevik October revolution of 1917 attempts were made to change the seven-day week into a ten-day one. But these attempts failed to gain acceptance. A plan of this kind might sound logical in a world used to the decimal system. But it ignored the rhythm of life, the heartbeat of freedom. Even for people who want to settle down entirely in a secular life, the free day—the Sabbath, the Sunday—remains a gift. So to sanctify it—to "keep it holy"—is an excellent task for every Christian and every Christian congregation.

The commandment to keep the free day holy is immediately followed by the commandment for children to obey their parents—and for good measure, obedience to "the powers that be" is added at the same time. But this is far from the original meaning of the Fourth Commandment. Like all the commandments, it is primarily directed to grown-ups, not children. When we are told to honour father and mother, it means parents who have grown old and who are dependent on caring love. In a society with an increasing proportion of old people, a commandment of this kind is very much up to date. The relationship to those who are older brings out a fundamental principle of social humanity: the honouring that is meant here means loving, caring respect for those who are weaker. In that way, it is not far from the children, who are also dependent on love and care. Understood in this way, the commandment to respect children, which some people suggest should be an Eleventh Commandment, is already embodied in the ten we have.

Boundaries Secure Freedom

Even if the Ten Commandments are interpreted as a signpost to freedom, they undoubtedly set boundaries: "You shall not . . . you shall not." It is true: to secure freedom also means to observe boundaries. The idea that freedom is boundless is no more than a dream. One of the most popular songs by the German songwriter Reinhard Mey maintains that "over the clouds freedom must surely be limitless." But although human beings have learned to fly, life is still lived on earth: in a limited space, in limited freedom.

Yet if we look more closely, these boundaries do not restrict freedom; they make it possible. This becomes particularly clear from the Fifth Commandment: "You shall not kill." It is only where the integrity of human life is preserved that talk about freedom is possible at all. Consequently, the uninfringeability of human life is a precious possession; to take another person's life intentionally or through negligence is outlawed.

Nevertheless the dispute about the scope of the prohibition against killing continually flares up afresh. New medical possibilities raise the question about the protection of unborn life. Is it permissible to select from among artificially produced embryos the ones that are to be implanted in the mother? Is it permissible to end an unplanned pregnancy?

And what if a diagnosis during pregnancy points to a genetic defect? Such questions are not easily answered. In our thinking about them, Christian ethics contributes the conviction that the human being is designed to be the image of God. We cannot willfully dispose of even developing human life, for it is not merely an object.

Similar questions arise at the end of life. Is it permissible in the case of incurable illnesses to discontinue life-prolonging measures? Is it permissible to end human life through active euthanasia? The biblical commandment enjoins us to answer questions of this kind in light of the priority to be given to life. Dying has its time, just as has life. Dying must be permitted when it is time; to prolong life under all circumstances does not minister to life. Yet here we must distinguish the demand for medical assistance in the case of suicide, or the justification of death on demand, because in these cases death becomes a human act. And that would infringe the very core of the medical ethos, which is directed toward the preservation of life—toward helping and healing.

Side by side with the integrity of human life stands the integrity of human relationships. Reliability and responsibility are essential for all human relationships. But the most intensive relationship between two human beings is marriage. So to intervene in it, or to break out of it behind the partner's back, is a betrayal. The changing forms of living we are experiencing does not alter this fundamental insight. Relationships can break down; in situations where there is no way out all that remains is to admit the failure. But enduring partnerships must not be wantonly broken up; that is and remains a breach of faithfulness. How easily we human beings incline toward this is shown by Jesus' saying: "Let anyone among you who is without sin be the first to throw a stone" (John 8:7).

But at the same time Jesus radicalized the protection of marriage: "You have heard that it was said, 'You shall not commit adultery.' But I say to you that everyone who looks at a woman with lust has already committed adultery with her in his heart" (Matt. 5:27-28).

It is astonishing to see in what detail the Ten Commandments protect property. The Seventh Commandment forbids stealing. That reaches from the secret purloining of objects to the stealing of animals, and then to the robbing of another person's liberty. The scope of these inroads into the liberty of someone else reaches from street thieving to breaking and entering, and then to kidnapping.

The Ninth and Tenth Commandments forbid "coveting." The Bible understands by this every step—from the wish, to the planning, to the committing of an act that seizes possession of an object or a person to which one has no right. It is a matter of the unlawful acquisition, or unlawful use, of something belonging to someone else. Here the range is even wider than it is in the prohibition of adultery or theft. It now explicitly includes what we today call "the inviolability of the home." Transferred to today's conditions, legal tricks designed to cheat others of the basis of their livelihood are envisaged; tax fiddling, fraudulent subsidy claims, or corruption undoubtedly all fall within the scope of the Tenth Commandment.

The prohibition against "bearing false witness" has a special position. Its original context was a court proceeding. The person who, acting as a witness, says what is not true thereby endangers another person's life or the foundation of their existence. That is why this mean form of lying is particularly emphasized. Court proceedings show particularly clearly how closely truth and social solidarity go together.

This means that the duty to tell the truth is more than a matter of personal integrity. It springs from the responsibility for our common life. Of course, there is also a way of inquiring into the truth through which the life we share can be endangered or even destroyed. So no one is duty-bound to answer every question. What you say must be true, but not everything that is true has to be said. There is also a duty to keep silent. The person who infringes this duty destroys human relationships just as much as the person who deliberately lies. It is true that every lie is an offense against the honour of the partner to the conversation, but there are also questions that cannot be reconciled with the commandment to harm no one.

Perhaps that is the reason why we cannot simply find the sentence "You shall not lie" in the Ten Commandments. Here it might perhaps be better to formulate a commandment rather than a prohibition: "Always be sincere!"

The Ten Commandments do not comprise a comprehensive catalogue of moral behaviour. They do not solve all the problems about responsible action that arise today. But for that very reason they provide a good guide, because they link the assurance of freedom with its preservation. In this way the Ten Commandments safeguard human freedom. And that being so, they remain up to date, even in changing times. Every generation can learn from them. But in order to do so we must know what they are.

10. A Culture of Helping

One of them, a lawyer, asked [Jesus] a question to test him. "Teacher, which commandment is the greatest?" He said to him: "You shall love the Lord your God with all your heart, and with all your soul, and with all your mind" [Deut. 6:5]. This is the greatest and first commandment. And a second is like it: "You shall love your neighbour as yourself" [Lev. 19:18]. On these two commandments hang all the laws and the prophets."
—*Matthew 22:35-40*

Just then a lawyer stood up to test Jesus. "Teacher," he said, "what must I do to inherit eternal life?" He said to him, "What is written in the law? What do you read there?" He answered, "You shall love the Lord your God with all your heart, and with all your soul, and with all your strength, and with all your mind; and your neighbour as yourself" [Deut. 6:5; Lev. 19:18]. And he said to him, "You have given the right answer; do this, and you will live."

But wanting to justify himself, he asked Jesus; "And who is my neighbour?" Jesus replied: "A man was going down from Jerusalem to Jericho, and fell into the hands of robbers, who stripped him, beat him, and went away, leaving him half dead. Now by chance a priest was going down that road, and when he saw him, he passed by on the other side. So likewise a Levite, when he came to the place and saw him, passed by on the other side. But a Samaritan while traveling came near him; and when he saw him, he was moved with pity. He went to him and bandaged his wounds, having poured oil and wine on them. Then he put him on his own animal, brought him to an inn, and took care of him. The next day he took out two denarii, gave them to the innkeeper, and said, 'Take care of him; and when I come back I will repay you whatever more you spend.' Which of these three, do you think, was a neighbour to the man who fell into the hands of the robbers?" He said, "The one who showed him mercy." Jesus said to him, "Go and do likewise."

—*Luke 10:25-37*

Good Transportation

A day in Tanzania. The Lutheran bishops had gathered together for a conference, which I was permitted to attend as a guest. One of the items on the agenda was an unusual one: a pilot of the Mission Aviation Fellowship presented an offer from a not-for-profit airline. It was the first time I had heard about it. A few days later I was to experience the service of this unusual airline for the first time on a flight from Mboye to Dar-es-Salaam, in a four-seater aircraft. The Finnish pilot prayed before we took off, and told me about the country we were flying over during the flight.

Then one of this pilot's colleagues described to the assembled bishops the situations in which it is better for them to fly instead of embarking on a long journey alone by car. He finished his account with a reference to the parable of the good Samaritan, which he assumed would be familiar to the assembled bishops.

He asked whether they had ever noted the point of this parable—if they had ever noticed the difference between the Levite and the priest on the one hand, and the Samaritan on the other. The bishops were silent, for it was clear to them that the usual answers (the person who exercises practical neighbourly love is the truly devout person) wouldn't take them far. "The answer is obvious," said the pilot finally: "Good transportation, that is the important thing."

Then the scales fell from the bishops' eyes: the priest and the Levite were on foot when they passed the place where the man who had been beaten up by a robber and left half-dead was in need of help. The Samaritan, on the other hand, was a seasoned traveller who had a pack animal with him, on which he could carry the injured person to the nearest inn. He had at his disposal the means of making his neighbourly love effective: good transportation.

Neighbourly Love in Practical Form

After this encounter with a representative of the Mission Aviation Fellowship in Tanzania, I was often involved in discussions about whether neighbourly love is a practical matter or an unworldly affair. Jesus' story presents neighbourly love quite plausibly. Its point is not to expose the Levite and the priest, as some interpreters think when they interpret the story as a peg on which to hang their anticlerical prejudice. Whether the two men pass by out of cold-heartedness, or whether they are in a hurry to keep some appointment, or whether they feel helpless, being without wine, oil, and a pack animal—the story provides no answer to any of these questions. Everything comes down to the Samaritan, a man belonging to an ethnic group not much regarded by the Jews, a group with its own religious convictions and its own "holy mountain," Mount Gerizim. From the Jewish perspective he is somewhat of an outsider; but in Jesus' story he assumes the central position: he is the only one who knows how to help, and is prepared to do so.

Jesus' story is embedded in a dispute with a teacher of the law who wants to test Jesus. The lawyer asks him what one has to do in order to attain eternal life. Jesus points the questioner to the law, which the lawyer then cites in the summary form of the double commandment of love: "You shall love the Lord your God with all your heart, and with all your soul, and with all your strength, and with all your mind, and your neighbour as yourself." After Jesus has told him that this is the right answer, the law teacher counters: "But who is my neighbour?" So Jesus then tells the story about the Samaritan traveller who, unlike the priest and the Levite, comes to the help of the man at the side of the road who is in need, takes him to an inn, and looks after him, even overnight. Then he leaves him to the innkeeper, whom he pays for his services, promising that if further expenses are incurred he will recompense him on his next journey. Which of the three, Jesus asks the law teacher in closing, has been the neighbour to the one who had fallen victim to robbers? The lawyer answers: "The one who showed him mercy." Then Jesus answered: "So go and do likewise."

Jesus turns the initial question upside down: the lawyer had asked who was his neighbour. But Jesus puts a different question: Who became the neighbour of the person who had been attacked by robbers? I am showing neighbourly love when I am prepared to become the neighbour of someone else. That can even be a far-off neighbour; but it is pointless to declare neighbourly love to be absurd by maintaining that, after all, one cannot regard everyone as one's neighbour. The point is not how to find an alibi for oneself in the abstract, but how one can stand beside another person practically. It has nothing to do with the position of the person who needs help, or with the status of the helper. The real point is to perceive the other person as one's neighbour, and to do what is necessary.

A Culture of Helping

With the story about the good Samaritan, the spirit of unselfish helping has found an entry into our culture. The good Samaritan has become the model for people who go to the rescue wherever their help is needed, without asking whether it is to their own advantage. Rescue and nursing services or medical personnel know that they are committed to the model of the good Samaritan. Thanks to Jesus' story, the duty to help the person who cannot help himself has even made its way into our legal system: the failure to render help is a punishable offense. Everyone is duty-bound to give help in the case of accident, danger, or in some emergency if help is required, and if it can be expected of the individual concerned.

This is a graphic example showing that the impulses given by the Christian faith are not confined to the attitude of mind of individual Christians but have their effect on society—indeed, can even influence the legal system. Positive impulses of this kind have another side. They rouse protest where only selfishness is paramount and the spirit of love has no chance, where the culture of helping is pushed aside by the coldness of society, and where all that counts is what pays off. Christian faith passionately opposes developments of this kind—out of the passion called neighbourly love.

The Golden Rule and the Commandment of Love

In the New Testament we several times find the question of how the substance of the Old Testament commandments can be summed up. Two answers to this question are the most prominent. One is "the golden rule": "Do unto others as you would have them do unto you" (Matt. 7:12). The other puts the love of God together with love of one's neighbour. The two answers are not identical; it is, rather, that the one depends on the other.

"The golden rule" is the expression of an attitude of reciprocity. This comes out particularly clearly in the familiar and popular version of this rule: "Do as you would be done by." According to this version, reciprocity is the guideline enabling us to judge which actions we should avoid, that is, the actions to which we should not wish to be subject ourselves. But the golden rule goes further than this defensive ethic. It describes the guidelines to be applied to our own actions not just negatively but positively. However, this version, too, does not say what kind of expectations are in view. Of course, these expectations are not necessarily determined by pure egoism; the egoism is softened by the fact that I have to guide my own actions by what I expect of others. This reciprocity does not only set limits to what I do myself but, taken to its logical conclusion, also limits what I expect of other people.

And yet this attitude of reciprocity can be totally in accord with an atmosphere of cold calculation, and of "wait and see"—a "tit for tat" attitude. The ethic of the golden rule is not really determined by the spirit of the good Samaritan—even though it is certainly open for this spirit. For the double commandment of love goes beyond the spirit of pure reciprocity. Inherent in it is an element of uncalculated one-sidedness, of "prevenience"—of "running ahead." The Samaritan had compassion on the man who had fallen among thieves because he was "moved with pity" for him. In this he resembles the father in the parable of the son who was found again: he "had compassion" on the son when he saw him returning home.

Love doesn't calculate: it doesn't reckon with any return. That does not mean that love is without a return. Love that is returned and thereby fulfilled is certainly the greatest happiness a person can have. But anyone who makes love dependent on its being returned actually prevents any such a fulfilment from coming about.

Nevertheless, Jesus does not equate love with pure selflessness. With the biblical commandment, he reminds his hearers that we must say yes not only to other people but to ourselves as well: "You shall love your neighbour as yourself." The double yes, both to others and to oneself, is the heart of human life. This double yes is founded on God's great Yes to us and to our lives, and in that it is hidden and secure.

The sentences in which Jesus sees the biblical commandments as being summed up have again and again been called "the double commandment of love." But if we look at them closely, the two sentences that Jesus takes from the Old Testament and puts side by side are not really a double commandment; they are a triple one: love for God, love for our neighbour, and love for oneself belong together. They limit one another mutually, and point one another in the right direction. Those who love and trust God above all else will not idolize anything earthly but will glorify God alone. Those who love their neighbour will not put their own interests above all else but will align their lives toward what benefits other people. Those who love themselves will allow adequate space for attention to their own lives, and in doing so will renew the strength they need for their commitment to other people.

11. The Fellowship of Hope

I believe in the Holy Ghost,
the holy, catholic church,
the communion of saints,
the forgiveness of sins,
the resurrection of the dead,
and the life of the world to come.
Amen.
—*The Apostles' Creed, 2nd–4th century* CE, *Third Article*

I have a dream that one day this nation will rise up and live out the true meaning of its creed—we hold these truths to be self-evident: that all men are created equal. I have a dream that one day on the red hills of Georgia the sons of former slaves and the sons of former slave-owners will be able to sit down together at a table of brotherhood. I have a dream that one day even the state of Mississippi, a desert state, sweltering in the heat of injustice and oppression, will be transformed into an oasis of freedom and justice. I have a dream that my four little children will one day live in a nation where they will not be judged by the colour of their skin but by the content of their character. . . . When we allow freedom to ring, when we let it ring from every village and every hamlet, from every state and every city, we will be able to speed up that day when all of God's children, black men and white men, Jews and Gentiles, Protestants and Catholics, will be able to join hands and sing in the words of the old Negro spiritual: "Free at last! Free at last! Thank God Almighty, we are free at last!"

—*Martin Luther King Jr., speech at the March on Washington,*
  28 August 1963

The Death of a High Hope

I shall never forget the moment when I heard over the radio the news that Martin Luther King Jr. had been murdered. I can still remember where I was, and how I stood there as if rooted to the spot. Someone to whom people's hopes had been pinned—killed! A prophet of nonviolence—violently robbed of his life! The champion of black people, the defender of equal civil rights, the prophet of a new America would never be heard again. Would his great dream endure in spite of that? He had so touchingly exemplified it through his four children, who he hoped would one day no longer be judged by the colour of their skin but according to their character. Would the music of his life echo on, the music he had found in the spiritual that so extolled freedom: "Free at last! Free at last! Thank God almighty, we are free at last!"?

Much later, I came for the first time to Atlanta, where King grew up. I visited the house where his family lived, attended worship in the Ebenezer Baptist Church in Atlanta, Georgia, where he was pastor, like his father, and met Andrew Young, who like King had belonged to the Southern Christian Leadership Conference.

It was only after these personal encounters that I understood what tremendous courage Rosa Parks must have summoned up, when in 1955 in Montgomery she claimed a seat in the part of the bus reserved for whites, in order to strike a blow against the discrimination against black people in the southern states of America. The bus boycott that this sparked set on foot a movement, the goal of which was to be the same civil rights for all, regardless of race.

The Triumph of Reconciliation

It is only in retrospect that we can recognize the great line of tradition that runs from Mahatma Gandhi, the nonviolent fighter for Indian independence, by way of Martin Luther King Jr., the champion of equal civil rights irrespective of origin and race, down to Nelson Mandela, the first president of a free South Africa, which dared to make a new democratic beginning in truth and reconciliation.

Gandhi, King, Mandela—in the darkness of the 20th century each of them represents in his own way the political potentialities of neighbourly love. They use the chances open to nonviolent action. They show that politics in the spirit of the Sermon on the Mount are possible. The Hindu Mahatma Gandhi, the Baptist minister Martin Luther King Jr., and finally Nelson Mandela, who came from the ruling family of the Tembu and was the communist-oriented leader of the African National Congress (ANC)—these men were undoubtedly very different in background and character. With regard to the question of violence, too, each of them had his own attitude. But in the violence of 20th-century history all three ultimately became shining examples of the astonishing paths of nonviolence, examples of respect for their opponents, examples of the possibilities of reconciliation—in short, examples of the chances open to the Sermon on the Mount.

From them we see what power can be developed by the spirit of freedom, which, according to what the apostle Paul says, can be equated with the spirit of Jesus: "The Lord is the Spirit, and where the Spirit of the Lord is, there is freedom" (2 Cor. 3:17). Their example shows not only an alternative to the rule of force in the political sector. Their political breakthrough to the spirit of freedom also has a great impact on the understanding of the church as a community of men and women determined by this spirit of freedom.

A Fellowship of Hope

I still remember very well how astonished I was, when I was young, over some of the sermons I heard. The examples that the preachers used came from the women's group, or a church wedding, or from confirmation classes. I didn't find such a self-sufficient picture of the church convincing. I hoped for a Christian faith that radiated beyond itself, a community of faith aiming to effect something in society. Together with other people, I was interested in the transforming power of the Christian faith. For me, Bonhoeffer's idea about a "church for others" went together with King's later dream of a world in which "all of God's children, black men and white men, Jews and Gentiles, Protestants and Catholics, will be able to join hands."

In the Christian creed, faith in the efficacy of the Holy Spirit and a yes to the church as the fellowship of believers are followed by revolutionary hopes: for the forgiveness of sins, for the resurrection of the dead, and for eternal life. Even if these hopes point beyond all earthly experiences, they do not leave life within the confines of our earthly existence untouched. They lend wings to the dream of a shared life in which the

equal dignity of all human beings is realized without diminu-
tion, where there is a peace that does not depend on force but
on law, in which there is justice for every human being. The
great hopes of faith are fed by the confidence that the inven-
tive power of human beings does not have to destroy nature,
but can preserve it. The image of a "communion of saints" is
joined with the idea of a cooperation between the generations
that includes responsibility for the living conditions of the
people who will live after us. If we belong together with them
to "the communion of saints," we cannot be indifferent to the
world we leave behind us for them.

The future hope of the Christian faith points to a wide horizon of this kind. This wide horizon keeps the church open as a
fellowship of hope. It is time to interpret the church not only as
a remembering community but as a hoping community as well.
Of course, it is a community of remembrance. The Lord's Supper,
the Eucharist, to which Christians come together at all times
and in all places is a remembering meal: "Do this in remembrance of me." But this supper is simultaneously a meal of hope,
summed up in the acknowledgment: "Your death, O Lord, we
proclaim and your resurrection we praise, until you come in
glory." Between remembrance and hope, the fellowship of faith
is preserved in the celebration of worship and in the act of neighbourly love, in prayer and in the doing of the right, in the proclaimed word, and in service for our fellow human beings.

If this is the heart of every church, differences in our interpretation of the ministry or in liturgical tradition cannot in
the ultimate sense divide the churches from one another. If
every church is a fellowship of remembrance and hope, and
if the presence of every church is stamped by faith and love,
the common Christian bond must prove stronger than everything that divides us.

12. Turned to God and the World

We . . . are being thrown back all the way to the beginnings of our understanding. What reconciliation and redemption mean, rebirth and Holy Spirit, love for one's enemies, cross and resurrection, what it means to live in Christ and follow Christ, all that is so difficult and remote that we hardly dare to speak of it anymore. In these words and actions handed down to us, we sense something totally new and revolutionary, but we cannot yet grasp it and express it. This is our own fault. Our church has been fighting during these years only for its self-preservation, as if that were an end in itself. It has become incapable of bringing the word of reconciliation and redemption to humankind and to the world. So the words we used before must lose their power, be silenced, and we can be Christians today only in two ways, through prayer and in doing justice among human beings. . . . It is not for us to predict the day—but the day will come—when people will once more be called to speak the word of God in such a way that the world is changed and renewed. It will be in a new language, perhaps quite nonreligious language, but liberating and redeeming like Jesus' language, so that people will be alarmed and yet overcome by its power—the language of a new righteousness and truth, a language proclaiming that God makes peace with humankind and that God's kingdom is drawing near. "They shall fear and tremble because of all the good and all the prosperity I provide for them" (Jer. 33:9). Until then the Christian cause will be a quiet and hidden one, but there will be people who pray and do justice and wait for God's own time.

—*Dietrich Bonhoeffer, "Thoughts at the Baptism of Dietrich Wilhelm Rüdiger Bethge, 21 May 1944," in idem,* Letters and Papers from Prison, *trans. I. Best, et al., Dietrich Bonhoeffer Works (Minneapolis: Fortress Press, 2010), 8:389–90*

Return

In 1939 Dietrich Bonhoeffer returned home to Germany from New York after a stay of only a few weeks. He was 33 years old. He had been offered a post in the United States, an appointment that would have given him the chance to escape the military service in Hitler's army with which he was threatened, and which was against his conscience. By returning, he was throwing this chance away. Bonhoeffer had to be in Germany if he wanted to work for Hitler's overthrow and a new beginning. He was prepared to stand by his country in order to put an end to the crimes that were being practiced in that country's name.

After his return, friends procured for him the opportunity to work under Admiral Canaris in the foreign section of the military intelligence. This post freed him from military service. But above all, under its cover he participated in the plot against Hitler. His official job was to maintain contacts with ecumenical partners, and he used this position also to prepare for a new beginning after the dictator's overthrow. At the same time he worked on a book on theological ethics.

With his imprisonment on 5 April 1943 all these projects came to an end. It was several months before Bonhoeffer was able to come to terms with the disruption of imprisonment, and could turn again to theological subjects.

Breaking Out of the Religious Prison

During his months in the military detention prison in Berlin-Tegel, Bonhoeffer devoted intensive thought to the question of how the Christian faith can be freed from the prison of a religious language. For this language is an actual hindrance to the understanding of faith as a life-determining act and an attitude toward living. Religious language ties faith down to a segregated sector of reality. It sees faith as something inward, something separate from the world. And yet the core of the Christian faith is the becoming-human of God, that is to say, God's turn to human beings in the reality of their lives. Talk in the religious language to which we are accustomed does not meet this reality. Moreover, it turns the living God into "a God of the gaps": the sectors that have not yet been fully explained by modern science are reserved for God. God is supposed to go on being responsible for these gaps at least.

Bonhoeffer is convinced that this way of proceeding is doomed to failure. He unreservedly accepts that modern science has arrived at independence, accepting, too, its claim to understand the laws of nature and society. He sees this as so important a step toward enlightenment that he can talk, in lofty hyperbole, about "the world that has come of age" and about a human being who is also responsible through and through, and who is able to live without "God as a working hypothesis."

Bonhoeffer hopes that the result of this step will be a liberation for the Christian faith. For his concern is a Christianity that is lived in the world and enters into the worldliness of the world. But, of course, this cannot be a worldly faith robbed of its nucleus. It is, rather, a Christianity that concentrates on "the beginnings of understanding" and is thereby assured of its centre. The "religionless" interpretation he has in mind means turning above all to the important and central themes. But the great words of Christian faith—reconciliation and redemption, rebirth and Holy Spirit, forgiveness and love of our enemies, cross and resurrection—require an interpretation that is not confined to the domestic inner circle of people who are in any case convinced. Yet if we take a look outside, we see how incomprehensible the language has become that is often used in talking about these essential themes.

Great Words

Bonhoeffer's observations can still be endorsed today. Because the great words of Christian faith have become sealed up in a religious language, they are often presented only in banal form, even in the church's preaching. If there is talk about sin, hearers are reminded of the prevalence of traffic offenders; a chocolate bar is used to illustrate temptation. This actually blocks an understanding of the fact that sin and temptation are central themes in life; for this understanding is not communicated through trivial comparisons. They obstruct access to the new and revolutionary thing that comes into our world with the message of the gospel.

This world has become in a special way merciless, and therefore dependent on mercy and grace. In its dominant ideologies, it gives complete precedence to the maximizing of profits, and for that very reason it needs the insight that God is greater than all profit maximization.

In his time Bonhoeffer doubted the ability of the church to make people hear what is new and revolutionary in the Christian message. According to his assessment, the church is too much concerned with itself and the securing of is own existence. The decisive step to the necessary new beginning is the insight that the church is only the church of Jesus Christ when it sees itself as a church for others.

In the years that have passed since Bonhoeffer's death, many people have become aware that the preferential option for the poor is binding on the preaching and practice of the church. Going beyond Bonhoeffer, there is also a growing insight that for the sake of this option the church must make a claim on the strong as well and must galvanize intervention for justice and solidarity. But in spite of that, the degree to which the church is concerned with itself is still disturbing even today. Today, too, the recollection of the core of Christian existence presents us with a challenge. Bonhoeffer describes this core, this centre, by looking at people who "pray and do justice and wait for God's time."

Generally, this foundational formula is quoted only in abbreviated form: the future of Christian faith must consist of two things, prayer and the doing of right among human beings. This formula (which Bonhoeffer also used) is easy to grasp because it links up with an age-old description of the monastic life. It is governed by a double imperative: *ora et labora*—pray and work. This description of the monastic life, in its turn, picks up an ancient distinction between the contemplative and the active life. Bonhoeffer seems to take up this tradition once again; he only describes the purpose of Christian activity more exactly: its purpose is work for justice and freedom.

In God's Hand

Pray and work—Bonhoeffer ranges himself with this ancient Christian tradition. But he expands it in an important way. For him, it is not only two elements that belong to the practice of Christian life—prayer and the doing of justice or the right. There are three elements: prayer and work for righteousness, justice, and peace stand side by side with *the waiting for God's time*. Prayer and activity are joined with hope for what is to come. Although our prayer and what we do does not achieve everything we expect, that is no reason for resignation.

But neither is there any reason for arrogance. Through prayer and work, human beings do not force the future to be subjected to their rule; the future is still in God's hand. Bonhoeffer not only affirms the steps through which modern men and women have come of age; he wants at the same time to preserve them from a misunderstanding. He opposes the fantasies of almighty power that accompany progress in the scientific and technological domination over nature and society. The expansion of the potentialities for "effecting" things with the help of science and technology by no means makes human beings the lords and masters of the world. On the contrary, the expansion of their power goes together with new questions in which the future of humanity and the world again and again proves to be open and undetermined.

We can see examples enough today. Among them are crises in the financial markets and climate change, natural catastrophes and accidents in nuclear power stations, or the ethical challenges raised by the development of medicine and the life sciences. However far human power may reach, the future is not at human disposal. Whatever human beings take in hand never arrives at an ultimate perfection. The human being does not bring history to a close; history remains in God's hand. Modern men and women only remain "of age" if they remain aware of their limited power of implementation. They will only live up to their responsibility if they observe the limitation of their competence. And so, for a Christian attitude to life, waiting for God's time is just as fundamental as prayer and the doing of justice.

At the Side of the Suffering Christ

In Bonhoeffer's new theological beginning, respect for the maturity of the modern human being and criticism of the religious reduction of Christianity come together. The religious garment of Christianity must be laid aside for the sake of its substance. For this Bonhoeffer tries to find a language that, according to traditional standards, is perhaps unreligious but has a liberating and emancipating effect. He finds this language when he puts himself at the side of the suffering Christ. Here Bonhoeffer sees the essential theme of the New Testament. Jesus of Nazareth is brought before our eyes as the Son of God in whom God's love for us human beings is revealed. But this same Jesus is depicted as being helplessly exposed to suffering.

The helplessness of Christ in his suffering and on the cross becomes the pivot and central point for an understanding of God. It is only from this centre that it becomes possible to distinguish between Christianity and religion. This distinction, as Bonhoeffer says, "frees the gaze for the God of the Bible who acquires power and scope through his helplessness in the world."

This goes together with a clear idea about Christian existence. The place of faith is the world in its full "worldliness"—its entirety as life on earth. The faithfulness to the earth that is so clearly developed in the Old Testament is endorsed. In the becoming-human of Jesus, in his death on the cross and in his resurrection, the reality of God enters into the reality of the world: that is the fundamental insight. "Christians stand beside God in his suffering"—that determines the understanding of God as well as the understanding of human beings.

Just because of this concentration on God's suffering in the world, the distinctive mark of Christianity can be described in quite worldly terms. Here, down-to-earth dealings with circumstances as they are and with human weaknesses have their place, just as do respect for human endowments and the readiness not to accept everything just as it is. Bonhoeffer's attitude is expressed in the prayer written during those same years by his friend, the American theologian Reinhold Niebuhr:

> *God grant us the serenity to accept the things*
> *we cannot change,*
> *courage to change the things we can,*
> *and the wisdom to know the difference.*

13. The Seven Works of Mercy

When the Son of Man comes in his glory, and all the angels with him, then he will sit on the throne of his glory. All the nations will be gathered before him, and he will separate people one from another as a shepherd separates the sheep from the goats, and he will put the sheep at his right hand and the goats at the left. Then the king will say to those at his right hand, "Come, you that are blessed by my Father, inherit the kingdom prepared for you from the foundation of the world; for I was hungry and you gave me food, I was thirsty and you gave me something to drink, I was a stranger and you welcomed me, I was naked and you gave me clothing, I was sick and you took care of me, I was in prison and you visited me." Then the righteous will answer him, "Lord, when was it that we saw you hungry and gave you food, or thirsty and gave you something to drink? And when was it that we saw you a stranger and welcomed you, or naked and gave you clothing? And when was it that we saw you sick or in prison and visited you?" And the king will answer them, "Truly, I tell you, just as you did it to one of the least of these who are my members, you did it to me." Then he will say to those at his left hand, "You that are accursed, depart from me into the eternal fire prepared for the devil and his angels; for I was hungry and you gave me no food, I was thirsty and you gave me nothing to drink, I was a stranger and you did not welcome me, naked and you did not give me clothing, sick and in prison and you did not visit me." Then they also will answer, "Lord, when was it that we saw you hungry or thirsty or a stranger or naked or sick or in prison, and did not take care of you?" Then he will answer them, "Truly I tell you, just as you did not do it to one of the least of these, you did not do it to me." And they will go away into eternal punishment, but the righteous into eternal life.
—*Matthew 25:31-46*

Seven Works of Mercy

Martin of Tours was a 4th-century Christian. We are told that one day, at the gateway to the city of Amiens, he divided his cloak with a shivering beggar. It was only the following night that he learned what had happened. Jesus came to him in a dream, clothed with half his cloak, and said to him: "What you have done to the least of one of my brothers, you have done to me." Because of this saying, Jesus' discourse about the last judgment has become one of the foundational sayings of Christian faith. With its help people already discovered at the time of St. Martin that Jesus' sermon contains a catalogue of works of mercy: feeding the hungry, giving the thirsty something to drink, welcoming strangers, clothing the naked, supporting the sick, visiting prisoners. This list is repeated four times in our text, twice on the lips of the judging Son of Man, twice on the lips of the people who are judged, one group of them being saved, the other group condemned. In that early Christian era already, a seventh work was added to these six: burying the dead. Ever since then, the seven works of mercy have belonged to the core of the Christian faith. When we think about the influence of Christianity on world history, it is impossible to say anything more truly positive than this: that Christianity brought compassion into the world. For that very reason, there is nothing more distressing than the cases where people experience the opposite in the name of this same faith: violence instead of love, aggression instead of loving attention, abuse instead of mercy.

Of course, Christianity did not invent neighbourly love. We find parallels to the works of mercy in the Egyptian Book of the Dead, for example, as well as in Jewish traditions. But Matthew's Gospel gives the works of mercy as prominent a place as that which he gives to the Beatitudes. And so the ethic of compassionate help has moved into the centre of the Christian religion.

Elisabeth of Thuringia offers another example. The Hungarian princess lived at the beginning of the 13th century. She was widowed when she was only 20, and died at the age of 23. Her biography can be seen as a lived illustration of these works of mercy. Many people see a similar embodiment of mercy in Mother Teresa of Calcutta. Elisabeth of Thuringia and Mother Teresa saw themselves as disciples of Christ. The high rank given to Christian charitable help is based on the conviction that in the neighbour who needs my help Christ himself comes to meet me. So the discourse about the last judgment has remained to the present day a fundamental text for Christian charitable help.

Mercy and Politics

We have spoken of Martin of Tours, Elisabeth of Thuringia, and Mother Teresa. I will add another example, a very different one, which shows the reception history of this great text.

On Christmas Eve 1967, a group of protesting students stormed the Kaiser-Wilhelm-Gedächtnis church in Berlin. Their leader, Rudi Duschke, forced his way to the pulpit and unrolled this pronouncement from Matthew 25: "What you have done to one of the least of my brothers, you have done to me." He was pulled down from the pulpit, together with this biblical text, and was put out of the church. A disabled veteran even threatened him with his crutch.

This disturbance of the Christmas peace was met by outraged reactions. What this outrage left unnoticed was the question that had been asked so provocatively. Do the works of mercy have a political side? Is there a duty to exercise love through institutional structures—a question that was simultaneously being asked in the worldwide ecumenical community? Or, to turn the question upside down, does mercy turn into pure—indeed, false—almsgiving if unjust conditions allow people to go hungry, to fall sick, or to end up in prison? Is the discourse about the final judgment a call to political subversion?

Salvation and Judgment

For Christianity, Jesus' speech about the last judgment is a fundamental text. Generally speaking, only one of its main sentences is quoted: "What you have done to one of the least of my brothers and sisters, you have done to me." But parallel to it is another pronouncement that is given equal importance: "What you did not do to one of these least, you did not do to me."

About these two pronouncements opinions are divided. These two judgments divide human being into two groups, Whereas the one group is described as "those blessed by the Father" who "inherit the kingdom prepared for [them] from the foundation of the world," the others are cursed and given over to "the eternal fire prepared for the devil and his angels."

Isn't this a horror vision? People are judged not because they have committed some crime deserving of death, not because of sinful acts; they are delivered over to eternal damnation because they have left to themselves people who were in need of help. In the eyes of this Judge, what makes them "the lost" is not what they have done but what they have left undone. Those who neglect the works of mercy have no claim to mercy themselves.

We must not play down or trivialize the violent force of this conception. For a long time Christians believed in the reality of such a division. In medieval churches it was pictured in detail. When they know no other answer to violence and injustice, Christians have continually taken refuge in the certainty of an ultimate justice and have hoped that the evildoers—the Hitlers both great and small—would land up in hell.

When we think of the victims of injustice and violence these relentless ideas about a final judgment are understandable. And yet it is impossible to affirm the violence of these notions of faith. What is its outcome if it is transferred to our own behaviour? Then human beings arrogate to themselves the position of the heavenly Judge. Then force is legitimated, the death penalty justified, and the "just war" is considered by both sides to be possible. Then punitive methods of education and upbringing spread.

How many children have been mistreated because grown-ups set themselves up as judges? If we look at the cause of the widespread violence used against children and the attacks on young people, attitudes of this kind are what we meet. Consequently, the aggressive ideas that crop up at the centre of the Christian faith cannot be taboo.

The discourse about the last judgment expresses in pictorial form what is going to happen at the end of time: the sheep and the goats will be separated. The image probably means that the sheep will remain in the flock, whereas the young goats that are ready for slaughter will be removed from it, because they are destined for sacrifice. What we still find disconcerting here is that their separation as sacrificial animals is equated with a condemnation to eternal damnation. But the distinction between sheep and goats emphasizes the division into good and evil that runs through the whole discourse.

Christ—The Judge and Saviour for Everyone

The sinners are separated from the righteous, the works of mercy being the criterion for the separation—a separation made by "the Son of Man" who comes to judge at the end of time.

Here Jesus is linking up with the world of Old Testament ideas. He says that the Son of Man will come as King and universal Judge in order to gather "all the nations" before him.

In what does his judgment consist? It moves people's everyday life into the light of mercy. Consequently, this judgment sheds its light directly on that everyday life. It sharpens the conscience. The idea of judgment is a seed from which the concept of responsibility grows.

All earthly authorities to which we are duty-bound are provisional. If need be, we can try to escape them. But one authority has definitive authority: the Son of Man, before whom there is no cover-up. So we absorb into our lives the conviction that we are responsible to him; our consciences continually confront us with him. It is because this judgment is not simply deferred to the last day that conscience and responsibility have such great importance in the Christian view of the human being. The premise for the schooling of the conscience is the ultimate and absolute duty to render an account.

But what about damnation, which plays so important a part in the discourse about the last judgment? It is only endurable at all because it is Christ who is speaking, the Christ who, as we say in the creed, will come again to judge the living and the dead. When we think of him as Judge, we remember at the same time that he already took the judgment on himself: he did not shrink from death and took the path of damnation. It was he whom God exalted and in so doing appointed him to the office of Judge. He took the condemnation on himself, which means that in the judgment we can flee to him. If we hold fast to him, we can also rely on the fact that according to God's will "everyone shall be saved and come to the knowledge of the truth" (1 Tim. 2:4).

The Church, Too

We only grasp the full meaning of the sermon about the last judgment when we understand it self-critically. This self-criticism does not just affect the individual believer; it touches the community of believers as well. The church, too, stands before the judgment seat of Christ, and cannot put its own judgment stool in that place. The church, too, must face up to an ultimate responsibility for what it does and leaves undone. It doesn't just preach judgment to other people; it accepts that the same judgment applies to the church itself. If it knows that, it will not use judgment as a way of controlling souls, instead of ministering to the concern for souls. For the preaching of judgment is a demand for the rule of mercy. That is the only form of rule that is acceptable in a Christian church.

Wrong turnings taken by the church cause just as much shocked consternation as do examples of its self-righteousness. Only conversion can lead to renewal. It is only through conversion that human beings who have been damaged by abuse in the church and its cover-up can open themselves again for God's mercy. It is only then that they can also hear again the invitation for mercy among human beings. So the churches must be prepared for conversion themselves; for it is only then that new trust can grow.

The message is clear. At the end we shall be asked what we have done for the benefit of those who are weaker. The preferential option for the poor is the decisive criterion for what we do and leave undone. In an impressive rhetorical heightening, we are told which situations are meant: hunger and thirst, the alienation of the stranger, nakedness, sickness, and imprisonment.

Hungry

Hunger is the great theme of our rich world. Billions of people are living in absolute poverty—a statistic that expresses an inconceivable degree of humiliation, for the standard applied is one dollar per day.

We easily allow ourselves to be diverted from intervention on behalf of the hungry. Other tasks are pushed into the limelight: terrorism must be combated, the consequences of immoderate financial speculations and state mismanagement must be curbed. These undertakings are also urgent. But if the billions, and billions upon billions, which are made available to prevent bank bankruptcy, state bankruptcy, or unfettered speculation against the Euro or dollar were to be consistently employed to overcome poverty, we should live in a different world. If we were to take the debt relief of the poorest countries on earth just as seriously as we take the stability of the Eurozone or of North America, the poor of this world would have a better chance.

Women suffer most because this does not happen, for women bear the greatest burden of poverty. Sixty percent of unpaid work worldwide is performed by women; 70 percent of all the hungry are female; 80 percent of basic food-stuffs in developing countries are raised without payment by women. This ought to rouse us all, for human dignity is indivisible.

Thirsty

Thirst is mentioned, next to hunger. The first thing a baby does when it comes into the world is to cry and to drink. Thirst is a completely elemental expression of human physical need. Nothing is more worthy of compassion than a hungry mother with a child that is sucking at her empty breast. Clean drinking water is scarce, and is a precious possession. In the earth's poverty belt, many people do not have sufficient access to it. High infant mortality—nearly 25,000 children still die every day—is connected particularly with a lack of clean drinking water. Access to water is a theme of foremost importance in the context of political conflict. Control over water is control over people. As the Sermon on the Mount says, thirst is always a thirst for justice, too.

Alien

Sensibility for the situation of strangers is one of the basic features of the biblical message. Uprooted, homeless, searching for daily bread—that is the stranger's situation. Strangers are people who are pushed on to the margins of society, shut out without any chance to rise; strangers are children who have no language with which they can communicate, and young people who can now communicate only with the Internet; strangers are grown-ups who can no longer escape from what is cynically described as "careers in social assistance." In our society, the only people who are accepted are the ones who can produce certain qualifications; the others are dropped and don't belong. Added to this is often a lack of understanding of other cultures. But the insufficient integration of strangers is not just a cultural problem; it is above all a social one, and a problem about education.

Naked

Who among us still thinks about the danger of being left naked? In South Africa I came across this fear quite directly. A group of young people plunged into the waters of the Indian Ocean but none of them dared to take off t-shirt or jeans. They didn't trust anyone. Even if someone was supposed to keep an eye on their clothes, that person could, after all, make off with the lot himself. So they kept on what they were wearing, and at the end climbed into the bus that took them back to their township, wet through and shivering. Even at home they were unable to hang up their clothes to dry without keeping a watch over them; if a person doesn't want to be left naked, a watch has to be kept day and night.

The fear of having to stand there naked also takes very different forms. If teachers in boarding schools misuse their authority and force pupils to undress, this breaks through the protection of not having to expose ourselves naked to anyone else. Today, to clothe the naked must also mean to outlaw all the violations by means of which children and young people are forced to perform sexual acts, to pose for pornographic photos, or are misused in other ways. To clothe the naked means fighting against rape in all its forms. Solidarity with the victims demands that we resist these abusive beginnings and clothe the naked.

Sick

Standing by the sick: I am amazed at the down-to-earth character of this penitential sermon. Is there any greater misery than the loneliness of the sick and the old? They often die long before their deaths. For dying means sinking into a lack of relationship. Life is relationship. Lack of relationship is death.

We have confidence that death does not have the last word, because God holds fast to God's relationship with us beyond our deaths. But we disavow this confidence if we already leave people alone while they are still alive—clean and with enough to eat indeed, but with no one beside them. We need to give new importance to the family especially in this most humane of all undertakings: to stand by the sick and the old, and to free them from being without any relationship.

We also need to upgrade the value we attach to care. It is not just a matter of looking after people who need it; it is a matter of relationship. For this, time is required. What is also needed is a new appreciation of this profession, which is of central importance for the humanity of our society. I view it as an alarm signal that a statutory wage for the care sector is no longer a matter of course everywhere, so that a minimum wage becomes necessary. The dignity of caregivers and the dignity of those for whom they care cannot be separated.

Imprisoned

Another kind of isolation is explicitly stressed as well as sickness, and that is imprisonment. The churches have long recognized that it is important to visit people in prison and by so doing to make it easier for them to find a way back to a responsible life in liberty. Many people participate in this undertaking, both unpaid and professionally. But in this work of mercy another group is in view, too: people who have been deprived of freedom for the sake of their faith.

It was not only in the early Christian period that men and women who witnessed to their faith lived dangerously. Paul's imprisonments are a prominent example. Things are no different today. Often the people who are locked up because of their faith, and have to fear for life and limb, are nameless. Today it is Christians especially who are persecuted for reasons of faith and are deprived of their religious freedom.

I well remember someone who never tired of visiting the imprisoned, and that was Kurt Scharf, who was bishop of Berlin until 1976. Scharf felt that this was a duty to which he was called by Jesus himself. In the Nazi era he was pastor in Oranienburg, near Berlin. The concentration camp Sachsenhausen belonged to the area covered by his parish—at all events that was the way he saw it, much to the annoyance of the authorities. He tried as far as he possibly could to gain access to the people who were imprisoned. In later years he also visited men who had been condemned to many years of imprisonment for war crimes, as well as members of the terrorist Baader-Meinhof group. Some people saw what Scharf meant to be seen as an act of mercy as siding with the wrong people.

In South Korea he wanted to visit the theologian Ahn Byung-Mu, who had been imprisoned because of his resistance to the dictatorship. Without having received a visitor's permit, he set out on the long journey from Berlin to Seoul, the capital of South Korea. He was refused access to Ahn Byung-Mu, so without having fulfilled his purpose he returned home. But back home in Berlin, he found that the visitor's permit had arrived: it had intentionally been sent off too late. He immediately set off once more by plane and arrived for a visit that no one had expected any longer. This was a great encouragement for the whole South Korean opposition in those years. Scharf had taken on himself an enormously strenuous journey, but he had met Jesus, the Son of Man. "Whatever you have done to one of the least of my brothers or sisters, you have done to me."

The Dead

The discourse about the last judgment talks about six works of mercy. Early Christianity did not leave it at that. It added a seventh, the burial of the dead. They, of course, knew Jesus' disconcerting demand: "Let the dead bury their own dead; but as for you, go and proclaim the kingdom of God" (Luke 9:60). And yet they also knew that the turn from death to life includes a farewell to those who have died. When the Christians carried the dead to their graves, they were not turning their backs on the proclamation of the kingdom of God by doing so. They were proclaiming God's grace in the face of death. So no one ought to die unaccompanied, and no one ought to be buried unheeded. To accompany the dying and to accompany the dead to their final rest belong together.

Death does not have the last word. When people are given a Christian burial they are being entrusted to God. At their grave we hear the assurance that reaches beyond death:

> *What is sown is perishable, what is raised is*
> *imperishable.*
> *It is sown in dishonour, it is raised in glory.*
> *It is sown in weakness, it is raised in power.*
> *(1 Cor. 15:42-43)*

And at the grave a Christian congregation can sing the mediaeval hymn:

> *Jesus lives! Thy terrors now*
> *can no longer death appall us.*
> *Jesus lives! By this we know,*
> *thou, O grave, canst not enthrall us.*
> *Hallelujah!*

This certainty of the future in the face of death is not shaped by the notion that we human beings will live on after death just because of ourselves. We have hope beyond death because God holds us fast.

That being so, it is pointless to imagine what the future "resurrection body" will be like. In his first letter to the Corinthians Paul therefore intentionally chooses words that burst apart all our concepts. God has held fast to Christ—beyond his death on the cross. He holds us fast as well. So we can die confidently and give our dead into his hand.

This is why Christians bury the dead with reverence and revere their names, because at the end God will "receive [them] with honour" (Ps. 73:24). They look after their graves, to which they can go in their grief, and discover that in the course of time pain makes way for grateful remembrances.

All this has found an entry into Christian burial customs. These are by no means outmoded. It is true that burial customs are becoming more varied. There are burials in wooded places as well as in cemeteries. Because families are becoming scattered, anonymous burials are becoming more common. The old do not want to be a burden to anyone, so no one is to be left with the burden of their grave. That is understandable. And yet it is still right to have a place for the dead that is associated with their name.

> *Do not fear, for I have redeemed you;*
> *I have called you by name;*
> *you are mine. (Isa. 43:1)*

14. In God's Safekeeping

Our Father in heaven,
hallowed be your name.
Your kingdom come.
Your will be done, on earth as it is in heaven.
Give us this day our daily bread.
And forgive us our debts,
as we also have forgiven our debtors.
And do not bring us to the time of trial,
but rescue us from the evil one.
For the kingdom and the power and the glory are yours forever.
Amen.
—*Matthew 6:9-13; cf. Luke 11:2-4*

Our Father

The Christian faith takes varied forms, but in Jesus' prayer they are joined together. So to talk about the unity of Christian faith is not mere lip service. In this prayer it is reality. Ever since Christianity has existed, it has shared the Lord's Prayer. No moment passes in which it is not being prayed somewhere or other on earth. "As o'er each continent and island / the dawn leads on another day, / the voice of prayer is never silent, / nor dies the note of praise away."

The Lord's Prayer is a poetic text that brings us close to Jesus and to his own time and language. For if it is translated back into Aramaic, the language Jesus himself spoke, it emerges that the short lines of this prayer were rhymed. Compared with the wordiness of many other prayers it is refreshingly short. In the Gospel of Luke it even comprises only five petitions, not seven as in Matthew.

Many people are familiar with the Lord's Prayer, so a frequent reproach is that it is prayed unthinkingly. The philosopher Friedrich Nietzsche even maintained that "the prayer has been invented for people who really have no ideas of their own." In his rebellion against the faith of his forefathers, Nietzsche had evidently forgotten that familiar words and their repetition is an important element in religion. It gives a sense of home.

Associated with the Lord's Prayer is the idea that—like the rosary, for example—it is prayed unceasingly. In Germany in the 19th century, it even gave its name to an open lift or elevator: the *paternoster*—the "Our Father." The lift, supported by two steel cables, revolves unceasingly, and passengers can step in or out at any floor during its progress without the lift's having to be halted. It is relatively slow, but it has an unequalled transport capacity.

It is not blasphemous to call a lift after the first words of the Lord's Prayer. On the contrary, the name is an important pointer. Short though it is, or rather just because of its brevity, Jesus' prayer can carry many people along with it. One can enter into it at any one of its petitions. Every time one prays it, a different sentence can become particularly important. One can even go beyond the sequence of its clauses, and pray it from back to front.

The Lord's Prayer is familiar to many people. But it begins with a surprise. It is anything but a matter of course to address God as "Father." This address is sometimes called in question, because it is misunderstood in the sense of a male picture of God. But this is countered by clear utterances in the Bible that ascribe motherly characteristics to God, too: "As a mother comforts her child, so I will comfort you" (Isa. 66:13). But the address is surprising above all because it turns to God so intimately and trustingly. Jesus prepared the way for this, for we are told that he always addressed God as his Father. Even in his greatest despair, in the garden of Gethsemane, this was the way he chose to address God: "My Father, if it is possible, let this cup pass from me; yet not what I want but what you want" (Matt. 26:39). But in the prayer, the title of Father is expanded. When God is addressed as Father "in heaven," God is being distinguished from all earthly fathers. It is not a general father image that is being transferred to God; but in divine uniqueness God is given a trust that can be compared with the trust given to one's own bodily father.

The Glory of God

The Lord's Prayer is clearly structured. The address is followed by three petitions that ask God to do what God wills should be done. Then come four petitions that talk about the "we" of us human beings, and our needs. The prayer ends with the praise of God.

At the beginning stands the "hallowing"—the calling holy—of God's name. God enacts this sanctification. God presents Godself to Abraham and to Moses as: I am the Almighty, I am the Lord, I shall be who I shall be. Because God calls God's own name holy, human beings turn to God in reverence when they "call upon the name of the Lord," as the phrase goes. The fact that human beings should not misuse the name of God—indeed, according to Jewish tradition, should not even pronounce it—is in itself only a pale reflection of the fact that God is concerned for the divine name to be kept holy. Here the name stands for the person. God "hallows" the divine name in God's creative activity as well as in God's gracious turning to the world. God hallows the divine name by coming close to the human race in Jesus Christ.

The reminder that human beings and the world are hidden within the name of God is the heading over every service of worship. So worship begins in the name of the triune God. But this can also be said of everyday meetings, which end with "goodbye" ("God be with you"), and in earlier times finished with "adieu" (à *Dieu*). It is sometimes only a short step from the thoughtlessness with which such turns of phrase are used to their misuse. German soldiers used to have "God with us" engraved on the buckles of their belts, and associated with this the conviction that God would bring them victory and would defeat their opponents. It also sounds arrogant if any particular land is described as "God's own country," as if the whole world did not belong to God: "The earth is the LORD's and all that is in it, the world, and those who live in it" (Ps. 24:1).

The horizon for the hallowing of God's name is the world. The whole world is intended to show that God's is the glory and that God's name should not be misused. What God has created is to be reverenced everywhere in the world. But in reality we are removed from this. The world is still not redeemed. The kingdom is still to come. God's glory is still veiled. "Your kingdom come." That is the shortest petition of all. But out of it speaks a great longing, out of which we hear the hope that

God's righteousness and justice will prevail, and that God's peace will rule.

An old man sits among the ruins of his life. On 11 March 2011 his house was overwhelmed by the wave of the Japanese tsunami. The man says that he is praying that in the end everything will come right. "Your kingdom come." The prayer breaks through the vicious circle that seems to have closed in the ruins of the catastrophe. It is reminiscent of the words of one of the psalms: "Save me, O God, for the waters have come up to my neck. I sink in deep mire, where there is no foothold; I have come into deep waters, and the flood sweeps over me. . . . O God, in the abundance of your steadfast love, answer me. With your faithful help rescue me." (Ps. 69:1f-2, 13).

The world in which we live is God's creation. But it is not an idyll. It is full of dynamism. It provides space for the beautiful things that we enjoy and for the good things that can develop. But its forces can also be destructive. It is not only human beings who act violently; nature can be violent, too. God has conceded nature, with its natural laws, its own rights; and God has entrusted us human beings with liberty. So we pray that God will preserve the world for a future in which righteousness, justice, and peace will rule.

To let God's will be done in the conflicts and contradictions of our world is not easy. Sometimes I am plagued by doubts as to whether what other people say is God's will really is God's will. Does God really want suffering and death? Whenever I remember God's demand to Abraham to sacrifice his son Isaac (Gen. 22:2), I am bewildered. I feel equally rebellious when I come to Jesus' prayer in the garden of Gethsemane that the cup of suffering might pass him by (Matt. 26:39). We need to find space in prayer for this rebellion. The prayer that God's will may prevail includes this kind of struggle. In this petition we cannot ignore the gas chambers in Auschwitz or the prison cells on Robben Island or in Guantanamo. We have to decide whether we want to see in them God's will or its exact opposite. According to Martin Luther's pugnacious view, this petition includes the plea that God will strike back at his adversaries, among whom Luther explicitly names not just the devil and the tyrants but bishops and heretics, too. But in this way of course the naming of God's will can also be misused—not as submission to what seems to be unalterable, but in a struggle against those we don't like, who are to be polished off in the name of God.

In asking what the will of God is, Christians hold fast to the only image of God they know: the suffering and dying Christ. The inward struggle with his fate in the garden of Gethsemane ends precisely in the prayer that he teaches his disciples in the Lord's Prayer: "Your will be done" (Matt. 26:42). He sacrifices his life and prays to God for grace. In divine compassion, God shows that compassion is what God wants. So the appeal to God's will involves a critical potential. It is not suited to justify crusades or the restriction of freedom. It is an encouragement to empathy with the suffering, and to walk with head held high.

Here again, as in the name with which God is addressed, it is more than the earth which is in view. God's will is to be done "on earth as it is in heaven." According to the picture language of the Bible, heaven is the place where God rules, so it is also called "the kingdom of heaven." What makes this prayer a bold one is not the plea that God's will may be done in heaven but that it may be done on earth as well. That presupposes that God will make the divine will prevail on earth, too. It is just here that the prayer leads into the centre of the Christian faith. For that faith is determined by the conviction that

God leaves the heavenly throne and becomes a mortal human being. It is too little to say that Christianity, like Judaism and Islam, is "a book religion." What is much more important is that it is a religion of incarnation. God commits Godself to finite, mortal life on earth. The eternal God enters into God's own experience with time. And by doing so God makes the divine will prevail—on earth as in heaven.

The Neediness of Human Beings

There is a marked break in the Lord's Prayer, an abrupt transition from the petitions addressed to God (God's name, kingdom, and will) to the group of petitions that look at human beings. The prayer now ceases to talk about "your name, your kingdom, your will"; it now has to do with us: our daily bread, our guilt, and the people who have incurred guilt toward us, our evil, and our temptation. Three petitions that are turned toward God are followed by four where the theme is human need.

The first of them has to do with the means of maintaining life. In early Christianity, the prayer for daily bread was related to the celebration of the Last Supper, and the conclusion drawn was that the Eucharist could not be too often celebrated. But what is really meant is our daily food in the widest sense. The petition derives from a world in which bread was offered at every meal. It is very probable that here daily bread means sustenance for the following day. "Give us today our bread for tomorrow" is the way we might render this petition.

Does this conjure up the spirit of anxiety that in another context Jesus clearly rejects? In the Sermon on the Mount he explicitly warns us against worrying about the next day; it is enough if each day has is own trials (Matt. 6:34). To look toward the rule of God counteracts an anxious revolving round one's own future; for it is only in this rule that human beings find peace and assurance. It only seems that the prayer for daily bread in the Lord's Prayer is in tension with this. Fearful anxiety is not recommended, nor is the prayer for daily bread in line with the idea that, through far-seeing planning, ultimate security for one's own life can be achieved. It is rather that the prayer breaks away from a rotation around one's own future. It is an invitation to a trust in God in which provision for the next day can also have its proper place. What is being thought of here is not just the individual who has to look after him- or herself. It is a matter of the necessary livelihood for families and large households, which cannot be secured without a certain degree of responsible looking ahead. The serene certainty that this petition breathes is all the more important. It is appropriate that it should stand exactly in the middle of the seven petitions that make up the Lord's Prayer.

The next petition begins with the word *and*. The forgiveness of guilt is as important as daily bread. This guilt is viewed in quite down-to-earth terms, which is why the word used is the same as the one employed for financial obligations. This is the only context in which the prayer mentions not just a divine action but a human one, too. Pardoning and forgiving are so central if shared human life is to be successful that they are explicitly mentioned. When something blameworthy occurs between human beings, a relationship can be lastingly spoilt and hopelessly destroyed. If guilt cannot be addressed, this guilt cannot be surmounted. Where it is not admitted and deplored, forgiveness has no starting point. But when it is admitted, a new beginning becomes possible. This opportunity to begin afresh is one of the great miracles in human life. And it is as necessary as daily bread.

Our experience in our dealings with other people finds a direct correspondence in our relationship to God. Our guilt toward God consists of our notion that we always know best and are not dependent on God. To want to be like God is the beginning of our human lack of orientation. That is why Martin Luther called the person who cuts him- or herself off from God "a self-warped person." The forgiveness of guilt can free us from this tension. It frees our gaze for faith, hope, and love. Jesus' prayer gives us the courage for this attitude toward living.

It also shows that it is not possible for human beings to do away with guilt completely, just by themselves. No forgiveness that we confer on each other makes the past undone. As human beings we remain so involved in each other that the one is indebted to the other. We are also freed from the notion that we can overcome the past by "maximizing" everything possible into the future—whether it be through an increase in technological achievements, material profits, intervention on behalf of other people, or the enjoyment of life. This idea about the future makes progress an absolute and ideological identity, although progress is always fragmentary and threatened by setbacks. Yet however triumphant, no progress blots out the past. That is better left in God's hands than confided to human faith in progress. Trust in God's reconciliation opens the path for recollecting solidarity with the victims of past guilt.

The plea for forgiveness is followed by the plea to be spared temptations. What kind of temptations are meant here? And who is the tempter? The devil, as in the story about the threefold temptation of Jesus in the wilderness (Matthew 4)? Or God's own self, as in the sacrifice of Isaac (Genesis 22)? The New Testament talks especially insistently about the temptations of the end time, the trials that precede the coming of the kingdom of God. There is much to suggest that the temptations which the sixth petition in the Lord's Prayer talks about should be differentiated from the evil with which the prayer concludes. So are the "temptations" trials imposed on human beings by God?

How are we to find a way of understanding this in a time when temptations are seen rather in terms of a cheesecake, alcohol, or a sexual infidelity? In these cases, to invoke God is inappropriate. It is, rather, a question of not giving way to one's own impulses at the cost of other people and one's own health. Those who lack the necessary sense of responsibility for others and themselves cannot justify this by declaring that God was simply putting them to the test. Trials of this kind rather have to do with the great challenges in life over which we ourselves cannot dispose. I am faced with some great responsibility that threatens to be beyond my strength without my being able to escape it. I fall ill, and all my plans are overthrown. In some great misfortune people need a comfort that I myself cannot provide. A natural catastrophe, a war, or an inhumane dictatorship raise the question: How can God can permit this? All these are trials with which God faces us. We hope that we may be preserved from them. And if not, we ask God to give us the strength to bear them. We have confidence that God can do so. For God has exposed the divine self to such trials, to the point of death on the cross.

But in the contradictions and conflicts of our lives we encounter not only divine trials and testings; we also run up against the power of evil. Human beings have continually imagined this power in person and as a person. But for all that, there is no article of faith in the Christian creed that envisages belief in the devil. Yet to be blind to the power of evil would be an unforgivable foolishness. For it shows itself in the bodily pain we suffer, but also in the moral transgressions of which we ourselves are just as capable as other people.

These physical and moral forms of evil bring us up against a fundamental problem. For our lives are marked by the painful experience that God is not as yet all in all. It is for that very reason that it is so important to look beyond the evil and not to leave evil the last word. So the final petition looks forward to the future redemption in which evil will no longer have any power. This anticipation of a good future already confers here and now the power to put evil in its place, to resist it, and to stand by the victims of evil happenings. In this way the future for which we hope shows itself to be a power in the present.

The Future as the Power of the Present

The Lord's Prayer ends with the praise of God. God's praise is the form in which the future is drawn into the present. That enlivens our sensibility for the good that can already be experienced and given a form here and now. In what is good we see a reflection of the kingdom, the power and the glory with which God's eternity is completely and utterly fulfilled.

At the centre of these three exuberant phrases stands the force, the energy, which inspires the confidence that the seven petitions of the Lord's Prayer will not come to nothing. Those who pray know themselves to be borne up by the certainty that God's Spirit brings into being a bond that joins us to the source of this force and energy. The prayer does not end by drawing up a balance sheet of our own capacities; it ends in a trust that goes beyond them. The person who praises God with these words is confident that God's Spirit transforms the world. This transformation is possible because God says Yes to this world. God's Yes to this world has a name: its name is Jesus Christ. To this Yes of God's, Christians respond with their own Amen (2 Cor. 1:20), in which they say: so it is and so it will remain.

Conclusion: And Now Faith, Hope, and Love Abide, These Three

If I speak with the tongues of mortals and of angels, but do not have love, I am a noisy gong or a clanging cymbal. And if I have prophetic powers, and understand all mysteries and all knowledge, and if I have all faith, so as to remove mountains, but do not have love, I am nothing. If I give away all my possessions, and if I hand over my body to be burned, but do not have love I gain nothing.

Love is patient; love is kind; love is not envious or boastful or arrogant or rude. It does not insist on its own way; it is not irritable or resentful; it does not rejoice in wrongdoing, but rejoices in the truth. It bears all things, believes all things, hopes all things, endures all things.

Love never ends. But as for prophecies, they will come to an end; as for tongues, they will cease; as for knowledge, it will come to an end. For we know only in part, and we prophesy only in part; but when the complete comes, the partial will come to an end. When I was a child, I spoke like a child, I thought like a child, I reasoned like a child; when I became an adult, I put an end to childish ways. For now we see in a mirror, dimly, but then we will see face to face. Now I know only in part, then I will know fully, even as I have been fully known.

And now faith, hope, and love abide, these three; and the greatest of these is love.

—*1 Corinthians 13*

Love until Death—A Farewell Love Letter

And now, dear heart, I come to you. I haven't added your name to any list because you, dear heart, have a quite different place from all the others. For you are not just a way God has used to make me what I am. No, you are me myself. You are my thirteenth chapter of First Corinthians. Without this chapter no one is a human being. Without you I would not have allowed myself to be given love. I took it from Mama for instance, gratefully, happily, as one is grateful for the sun that warms one. But without you, dear heart, "I would have not love." I am not saying that I love you—that's not it. It is rather that you are the part of me without which I should be incomplete. It is good that I lack it, for if I had it as you have, this greatest of all gifts, my dearest heart, I should not have been able to do many things—then many an appropriate step would have been impossible, then I should not have been able to face in this way the suffering I have had to face, and much else. It is only together that we are a human being. We are . . . a single creation idea. That is true, literally true. And so, dear heart, I am completely sure that you will not lose me on this earth, not for a moment. And after all it is this which we were also permitted to symbolize through the Lord's Supper in which we were together, and which has turned out to be my last.

I have wept a little, but not sadly, not wistfully, not because I would like to go back—no, out of gratitude and trembling humility over this documentation of God's. It is not given us to see him face to face, but we must surely be greatly moved when we all at once realize that he has gone before us our whole life long as a cloud by day and a pillar of fire by night, and that we are permitted to see that suddenly, in a moment. Now nothing more can happen.

But now, at the end, I say to you out of the treasure which has spoken through me and which fills this humble earthly vessel:

> *The grace of our Lord Jesus Christ and the love*
> *of God and the fellowship of the Holy Spirit be*
> *with you all. Amen.*

—Farewell letter written by Helmuth James von Moltke to his wife Freya after he had been condemned to death on 10/11 January 1944 for his participation in the assassination attempt on Hitler